Epicure

*Recipes
and More
for the
Curious Cook*

KATE BUSH, DAVID COBB, CHARLES OBERDORF & JANE RODMELL

Macmillan Canada
Toronto

Canadian Cataloguing in Publication Data
Cobb, David 1934–
   Epicure : recipes and more for the curious cook

Includes index.
ISBN 0-7715-9066-0

1. Cookery.   2. Food.   3. Dinners and dining.
I. Bush, Kate, 1948–   .   II. Rodmell, Jane, 1938–   .
III. Oberdorf, Charles.   IV. Title.

TX714.E65   1994   641.5   C94-931507-9

Macmillan Canada wishes to thank the Canada Council, the Ontario Arts Council and the Ontario Ministry of Culture and Communications for supporting its publishing program.

Front cover photograph, interior photographs: Robert Wigington
Cover design, interior design: Ken Rodmell

Macmillan Canada
A Division of Canada Publishing Corporation
Toronto, Canada

 2 3 4 5   98 97 96 95

Printed in Canada

For Joseph Hoare,
indispensable fifth wheel

Contents

Introduction

There is a communion of more than our bodies when bread is broken and wine drunk. And that is my answer, when people ask me: Why do you write about hunger, and not wars or love? — M.F.K. Fisher

OF MAKING MANY COOKBOOKS THERE IS NO END, AND MUCH study of them is a weariness of the flesh. Every year, maybe every week, rafts of new cookery advice float out onto treacherous seas, sails set for their special harbors, their particular culinary niches. Niches exist to be filled, but it says much for the restless inventiveness of cookery in our time that there are any still empty.

For ourselves, we aim to make an end run around the niches. As a four-headed team with the unholy crust to call ourselves Epicure, we have been writing since the early seventies about restaurants, food shops—and home cooking, from which these recipes are culled. Now in our third decade, we have been observers, a quadricephalic Mme Defarge, at a revolution of mind-bending proportions, as the *ancien régime* of North America's flaccid old eating habits rumbled past in the tumbrils. In a world shiftingly based on any number of uncertainty principles, anything is possible, but it is hard to believe that the next 20-odd years could conceivably produce change on so radical a scale.

February, 1973, when we first tucked in, was a slow month. In the U.S. the Watergate inquiry got gingerly under way. In Canada construction began on Toronto's CN Tower, tallest freestander on earth. The U.S. Treasury accused Canada of dumping aluminum. Wally Cox died. And Epicure, wet and squealing, cut our teeth on veal.

It was hardly a ground-breaking choice, but then North American cookery, both outside and inside the home, was only just starting to think again. Both sides of the border would have seemed to a visiting Venusian something like Rome circa 1100 AD—just coming out of the Dark Ages, crusades springing up everywhere, tiny perfect popes and antipopes, reform talk raging around fireside and colosseum, the vox pop thumping its chest and demanding better. In the food field it certainly got it, if not all at once. God knows it had taken long enough, but then the Dark Ages had lasted at least 500 years.

Every major North American city, of course, even back then, had fine places to eat, usually in exchange for financial pain. It is the norm that has changed, inside and outside the cities, and particularly in the home. What the hearth decrees the marketplace echoes, and the range of food and standard of its preparation, increasing out of all recognition, have resulted in an explosion of cooking diversity, ingenuity and invention. And in exchange, financial pain has these days to be searched out by those diners who perversely enjoy it.

The shift was ignited, no doubt, by the tsunami of immigrants to North America in this last quarter-century, throwing off specialized foodbooks and restaurants in their wake. Caribbean cooking, Latin American, Czech, Hungarian, Polish, Portuguese, Greek—above all, Asian: the local Chez Nous, so long the benchmark for style and standards, now seems an endangered species.

If immigrants provided the fuel for change, the engine was ready. Suspicion had grown that we are what we eat, as Brillat-Savarin advised 170 years ago, that what we were could stand a stiff dose of renewal and improvement, and that attention to our food, and the way we cooked it, should not necessarily be ceded to the professionals. These certainly have given it their best shot; as health, for example, became a matter for discussion in the home kitchen, restaurants strove to keep pace: health food, nouvelle cuisine, low-cholesterol, regional (hence somehow more genuine) cooking.

Much of this played into, or was guided by, the hands of fatuous foodies. Newness was all; fads came and went with the seasons. But anything that augured change was for the better after the long, dormant years: and so, spinach salads with bacon bits, shrimp chips, coulis, ancho chilies, raspberry's conversion into a salad dressing, swordfish, sun-dried tomatoes, extra virgin olive oil, balsamic vinegar, star fruit, pineau des charentes, ice wine, mineral waters, gravity-defying "elevations" on the plate and, depressingly often, huge platters with tiny portions, history's only dishes to starve and bankrupt at the same time.

In fact, as we all know, there is nothing truly new, or even nouvelle, under the sun. Consider this: "Modern cuisine, built on the foundations of the old, with less fuss, is simpler, cleaner and perhaps more knowledgeable." And this: "Today's dishes are very light, with a special delicacy and aroma. The secret has been discovered of how to eat more and to eat better, and to digest more rapidly.... The new cookery is conducive to health, good temper and long life."

Either could perfectly describe North America's current position in the cookery cycle; but the first was written by Frs. Brunoy and Bongeant, Jesuit priests, in 1739, the second 50 years later by Grimod de la Reynière, lawyer, author and critic (but who listed his occupation on his calling card simply as "gourmet" and died in 1837, as perhaps all gourmets should, right after Christmas dinner).

Where we go next is anyone's guess: after all the changing fads, low-density lipoprotein and Factor VII fears, fat-fights and wellness dogma, Epicure's minds are sufficiently muddled to have no idea. Our solace is that no-one else has any, either. Twenty years ago the North American food industry, intensely bullish and feeling its oats, forecast that by the end of the century we would all be consuming some 80 percent of our food away from home, for the most part in restaurants. At that time, the figure was about 25 percent and rising—it seemed to the industry thinkers—unstoppably. But by 1989, the figure had peaked at 40 percent; in1992 it had dropped below 35 percent; and now we're back to about where we were in 1974.

And why not? North America has been learning a new vocabulary for cooking at home, and if there is no such thing, strictly speaking, as North American cuisine, we have learned how to benefit from our great strength—the cross-cultural cooking, with the unequalled variety of international ingredients now available, that makes this continent the most excitingly varied place in the world to eat.

So, too, Toronto. When Epicure first set up a monthly stand in *Toronto Life* magazine, our city had long been the culinary butt of the continent, or anyway those bits of it that cared or even knew where Toronto was. Ten years later any sentient soul would have conceded that the city could at last be mentioned in the same (fairly long) breath as Montreal, New York, New Orleans, San Francisco and the rest of the big boys. A dozen years and a couple of World Series trophies later still, it's a question of how many of the big boys can be mentioned—for excellence, range and above all inter-national diversity—in the same culinary breath as us.

This is not mindless chauvinism; the change was in large part happily accidental and thanks to an exceptionally wide range of new immigrants, every last one of them appar-ently a gourmand, if not a gourmet. The United Nations Educational, Scientific and Cultural Organization (UNESCO) did not designate Toronto "the most ethnically diverse city in the world," as it did in 1989, without reason.

Still, it should be stressed that this is in no way a Toronto book. How could so catholic a collection of recipes be? Rather it is a distillation of some of our own favorite concoctions from the past 20 years. We came by them — usually not as a battalion but as single spies — from noshing travels and individual observations. In this time Epicure has, or have, sat in a tiny kitchen in Puebla, Mexico, watching the cook toss tortillas from hand to hand without missing a beat, and somehow (third hand) crushing endless green chilies for sauce; eaten 26 different varieties of exotic fruit during one mad 35-minute spell of excess among the fruit stands in the hills outside Caracas, Venezuela (a feat soon and justly punished); spent two months hitchhiking through Spain in search of the perfect paella, and found it in Tossa de Mar; sampled wild-boar prosciutto (deliciously gamey, once we got past the bristles) at the Peck market in Milan; been thunderstruck by the wondrously exotic selection of seafood and game on display at the KaDeWe in Berlin; stopped at every (actual count) roadside BBQ in Tennessee and Alabama in search of rib perfection (result: dead heat); eaten grilled cat's testicles at a roadside gypsy camp in the Pyrenees; drunk the world's worst mint juleps at the Kentucky Derby; sat on the shores of the Campbell River at April Point, British Columbia, as the sun went down and mighty planks of lightly cured sides of salmon smoked slowly over an open fire; eaten fresh Nova Scotia lobster and angus steak from Scotland at the Happy Valley Race Track Clubhouse in Hong Kong, sheep's eyeballs in Agadir, Morocco, eel stew at a Kyoto fish market and hot seaweed on toast (for breakfast!) in Oswestry, Wales; been so impressed with the flavors of the southwest that we consumed the whole menu (though not at one sitting) at Stephen Pyles's Tejas restaurant in Minneapolis; stumbled on a miraculous and untouched field of wild chanterelles near Killarney in northern Ontario, scooping up a couple of pails before black flies descended in ravening hordes, bent on reducing us to our component parts; gorged on pressed duck at the Tour d'Argent in Paris and been as impressed by the duck (Epicure's #, 94 years after they started numbering: 643,829) and supernal view overlooking the Seine as we were depressed by the rest of the food and the wretchedly rude service; wandered countless bazaars, sampling the world's best offal, sweet and endless, in Athens, fresh congrio in Santiago, bowls of crisp fried lima beans in Lima (and caught, somewhat breathlessly, fresh trout in Lake Titicaca at about 12,500 ft.); devoured crab in Chesapeake Bay and Sarasota, and in one gluttonous sitting at least 3 lbs. of fresh prawns, grilled just off the fishing boats in Dublin; wandered the hallowed halls of Emilia-Romagna where the best, the only, parmigiano reggiano is aged; learned how to barbecue whole small pigs, and decided the effort exceeded the reputation; and been incomprehensibly, possibly criminally, seduced by Liverpool's culinary wonder, the chip butty— french fries sandwiched between two pieces of flat bread, then slathered with a pail or two of butter and untold lashings of salt and pepper, all of which, by some recondite Liverpudlian alchemy, becomes an elutriative wonder, exponentially greater than the sum of its parts.

All of which respectfully submitted, if only to show that our sights, though aging, have been unconfined. Like joy.

Two last points. 1) This is intended to be a book not just for people who want to cook, but also for people who might like to ruminate on a few diversely discursive matters around and about what they're cooking with. A cookbook, in short, sailing among the sea of cookbooks, but sailing—we hope—alone. 2) Not long ago, four New York editors confessed over lunch that *at least one-third* of the recipes in the cookbooks that passed through their hands had not been tested by the people who wrote them. This strikes us as, in equal amounts, astounding and unforgivable.

And in this instance, be assured that it is also untrue. We have tasted every one of these dishes repeatedly; it is our urgent hope that you share our taste.

Eggs

CENT PER GRAM, THE EGG REPRESENTS THE GREATEST food value of our day, though there are times you could doubt it. For too long it has been the butt of fussy warnings, beloved of Wellness letters; high time to put the pieces together again.

Intact, the egg is as close to perfection as this world affords. Could anything so faultlessly designed be evil, or even wrong? Could anyone imagine, without Humpty Dumpty's example, something so fragile that a short sharp knock will shatter the shell, and so strong that, uncracked, it will withstand the effort of the strongest clenching fist?

And inside that shell the hen has managed to nurture something with the highest biological value of all common foods: low in calories (76 per 100 grams), high in protein; all the essential vitamins but one, plus impressive amounts of phosphorus and iron. An almost perfect food, then—add a glass of freshly squeezed orange juice to make up for the missing vitamin C and perfection is within your grasp.

Alas, the egg's P.R. problem, constantly dinned into us, is cholesterol, which the body makes anyway, and which, we are instructed, we should not take on much more of for fear our arteries silt up before their time, like the Mississippi Delta. Fear of Clogging has seen to it that we cut back on red meats, offal (brains contain four and a half times more cholesterol than eggs), butter and cream.

Eggs have taken the brunt; after all, we eat them in some form a few thousand times more often than we tuck into offal. Bacon and two eggs were once the only way to greet the day, but how often do we whip 'em up now? How often hear the reassuring short-order cries of "Two eggs up!" "One over easy!" "Adam and Eve on a raft?" Indeed, bacon and eggs have become *the* double-whammy no-no, until the next dietary Great Satan comes along.

What to do in the meantime?

Four options suggest themselves: (1) throw caution to the winds and continue eating eggs fried in bacon fat every morning (a.k.a. the Tomorrow We Die option); (2) eat only the cholesterol-free whites (drawback—the yolks may have the cholesterol but they also have the lion's share of protein, vitamins and *taste*; (3) switch to Egg Beaters, an ingenious chemical stew starring egg whites but a bit more interesting—is it the calcium pantothenate, perhaps, or the hint of pyridoxine hydrochloride?—than the whites alone. Drawbacks: as a liquid egg-on-the-plate substitute rather than cooking ingredient, Egg Beaters can only be scrambled or sandwich-fried. They're not marvelous on their own and cost about four times as much as the real thing.

And (4) moderation, which is boring only if common sense is. Except for those seriously into the cholesterol danger zone already, two to three eggs a week won't hurt, particularly given a reasonably active life. And take heart from this: thanks to less fat and more nutrients in their own diet, hens now lay eggs with 22 percent less cholesterol than they did in the early seventies, which ain't chickenfeed. Who knows? By the time you get to the last egg recipe here, some California farmer will probably raise a chicken on fresh air and mineral water that produces eggs with *100 percent* less cholesterol.

And taste like it.

A hen is only an egg's way of making another egg.
—Samuel Butler.

Sarah Bernhardt's Scrambled Eggs

The great actress was wont to say that her personal chef made the best scrambled eggs in the world. None could touch him, she averred. Yet he would never tell her what his secret was, and the divine Sarah went to her reward in 1923 still delighted by the eggs, but still in the dark. Here's the answer.

Eggs

Freshness is paramount. If fresh, when cracked and poured onto a frying pan, the white will cling steadfastly to the yolk and form a compact domed oval around it.

2 to 3 eggs

Salt and freshly ground pepper

1 tbsp. butter

1 clove garlic, peeled

Prepare and season eggs as you normally do in the scrambling mode. Melt butter in a pan and toss in eggs. Impale garlic clove with fork. Stir eggs with fork. Think what she must have been like as Hamlet! Serves 1 great actress.

Variation: The egg has immense possibilities when scrambled. Most seasoning is best gently folded in partway through the cooking process. In lieu of garlic, add 1 tbsp. cream to whisked eggs.
A purist will remove the nasty white strand attached to the yolk before scrambling.
Add chopped fresh coriander, parsley or basil; or roasted and peeled red and yellow peppers, and/or a dollop of soft goat cheese.
Smoked salmon is good as well, topped with some fresh dill or chives and salmon caviar.

Anyone can insult; the French insult with style.

Paris, the twenties: Hélène, Gertrude Stein's cook, has it in for Henri Matisse, the painter. Matisse, invited by Stein for dinner, checks with Hélène before accepting: what does she propose to cook? Hélène is furious: she might have forgiven a foreigner such gaucherie, but never a Frenchman.

Comes the day when Stein invites Matisse to dine a second time. Very well, says Hélène, through thin lips. In that case I'll not make an omelette, I'll fry the eggs. It takes the same number of eggs and the same amount of butter but it shows less respect. *And he will understand.*

Eggs on Toast with Mediterranean Vegetables

Fried eggs are commonly served on a tomato–based mixture in Spain (sofrito) and Mexico (huevos rancheros). Here's our version.

4 tbsp. fruity olive oil

2 cloves garlic, peeled and minced

1 onion, chopped

1 tbsp. seeded and finely chopped banana pepper

1 can (28 oz.) plum tomatoes, drained and chopped

1 bay leaf

1 cup chopped eggplant, end removed

1 cup chopped zucchini

1 cup chopped sweet red pepper

1 cup chopped sweet yellow pepper

1 cup mushrooms, sliced

1 tbsp. each finely chopped fresh basil and parsley

Lemon juice to taste

Salt and freshly ground pepper to taste

Scrambled eggs for 6

Buttered toast

An egg boiled very soft is not unwholesome.
—Jane Austen.

An egg which has succeeded in being fresh has done all that can reasonably be expected of it.
—Henry James.

In a large skillet, lightly sauté garlic, onion and banana pepper in oil. Stir in tomatoes and bay leaf; let stew for 5 minutes. Add eggplant; continue cooking 5 minutes. Add zucchini, yellow pepper, red pepper and mushrooms. Let the whole lot brew away until well softened, about 30 minutes. Stir in basil and parsley. Spike with lemon juice, salt and pepper. Pile scrambled eggs on buttered toast. Spoon tomato mixture on top, to the side or where you will.
Serves 6.

Variation: Let cooked mixture rest in frying pan. Break eggs on top. Cover and steam until eggs are set, approximately 10 minutes. Sprinkle with finely chopped parsley.

NASI GORENG

An Indonesian rice and egg dish. There is an exciting and unexpected taste: wonderful contrasts, of hot and cold, spicy and bland, and on it goes.

2 onions, minced

1 clove garlic, minced

2 chilies, minced or 1 tsp. hot chili paste

1/2 tsp. shrimp paste (optional)

3 tbsp. peanut oil

1/2 lb. medium shrimp, peeled

1/4 lb. ham, cut into strips

6 cups cooked long-grain rice

1 cucumber, sliced

3 tomatoes, sliced

4 eggs, fried, sunny-sideup

1 tbsp. chopped coriander

Blend onions, garlic, chilies and shrimp paste in a blender or food processor to make a fine paste. Heat oil in a large, heavy skillet over medium heat. Add onion mixture; cook 5 minutes stirring constantly. Throw in shrimp and ham; cook briskly. Stir in rice; toss until hot and coated with sauce. To serve: Circle a large platter with cucumber and tomato slices. Pile rice in center. Top with eggs; scatter the whole lot with coriander.

Serves 4.

Adding an egg or two to any dish, hot or cold, that looks unpromising, or lacks substance, or tastes unfulfilled, will bring it instantly to life. This is called the Lazarus principle, possibly the greatest of the egg's many miracles.

You could shout it till you're blue in the face for all the good it does, but *there is no nutritional difference between a white egg and a brown one.* White-shelled eggs are laid primarily by White Leghorns, browns by Rhode Island Reds; that is all. The RIRs require a slightly more varied feed, which means their eggs sometimes cost more. Brown eggs *look* healthier—whole wheat vs. white—and the idea that they're more ecologically and nutritionally sound, the very Volvos of eggdom, dies hard.

CREAM-CHEESE PANCAKES FOR CAVIAR AND SMOKED SALMON

Delightfully light.

4 eggs

1 cup cream cheese

1/2 cup all-purpose flour

1/2 tsp. salt

1/4 cup milk

1 tbsp. finely chopped fresh dill

2 tsp. clarified butter, melted

1 cup fresh cream cheese or crème fraîche (*see below*)

1 1/2 lb. smoked salmon

1 oz. salmon caviar

Fresh dill sprigs and lemon juice for garnish

Freshly ground pepper

*The bravest chief
that ever fought,
The lowest thief that
e'er was caught,
The harlot's lip, the
maiden's leg,
They each and all
came from an egg.
—Clarence Day.*

*Beat eggs until frothy. Add cream cheese and mix well. Sift together flour and salt; beat into egg mixture, alternating with milk. Heat a large heavy skillet over medium heat; brush with clarified butter. Using a small ladle, pour enough batter to make thin pancakes 2 inches wide. Cook 1 minute. Flip and brown lightly on the other side. Repeat until all batter has been used. To serve, arrange pancakes on a large platter. Place a dollop of cream cheese or crème fraîche on each pancake; top with smoked salmon and salmon caviar. Garnish with dill and a squeeze of lemon juice. Serve with freshly ground pepper.
Makes 48 pancakes.*

Tip: Prepare pancakes several days ahead. Wrap and freeze. Reheat at 250°F, wrapped in foil, 10 minutes. May also be prepared a day before, wrapped and refrigerated. These little pancakes are also superb with yogurt or sour cream and fresh fruit.

Crème Fraîche

Increasingly popular naturally matured, slightly sour, raw cream is much prized in Europe by cooks for the rich sharpness it adds to soups, sauces and salad dressings. A facsimile using pasteurized cream: mix 1 cup 35% cream with 1 tsp. buttermilk. Pour into a jar and let stand in a warm place until thickened, approximately 24 hours. Stir gently, then refrigerate, covered, 24 hours before using.
Makes 1 cup.

Soups and Chowders

SOUPS

SOUP, THAT MOST BASIC OF FOODS, HAS BEEN AROUND since the discovery of fire by Paleolithic man: what's easier or more economical than throwing some grains or greens or leftovers into a pot and boiling them to make them digestible?

Soup as we know it dates from the end of the Dark Ages, when it became a European staple. The word itself comes from *sopp* or *sup*, which was actually the bread the cook poured the broth onto, to give it more body. It also supplied the means to get the most out of the juicy bits for those who had no spoons.

Come today, when we have the spoons and tend to do without the bread but still want the most out of the juicy bits. For good digestive and health-repairing reasons, we mostly take our soups hot—"Cold soup is a very tricky thing," Fran Lebowitz rightly observed, adding that it sometimes gives the impression that if one had only arrived on time it might have been a whole lot warmer—and the trick is to balance its content in the context of the meal. Too often, soup is made for guests because the cook feels guiltily that it *should* be made, a makeweight for the meal as a whole. "This'll keep 'em quiet," she thinks, throwing something haphazard together; and turns her more earnest attentions towards the other courses.

Result, in pinball parlance, *TILT*—imbalance, and probably an unstated curiosity among the guests as to why she bothered. Here are some recipes to bother about but not to be bothered by.

CLASSIC ONION SOUP

This robust soup remains the best of onion soups. A popular variation these days is to substitute cider for 2 cups of stock and to use Oka cheese in place of Swiss. The most important part of this soup is the stock.

4 tbsp. butter

2 Spanish onions, thinly sliced

1 tbsp. sugar

2 tbsp. all-purpose flour

8 cups warm brown stock (*recipe follows*)

2 tbsp. brandy (optional)

16 1/2-inch slices French bread

2 cups shredded Swiss cheese

In a large heavy pot, sauté onions in butter until soft. Add sugar; cook until onions are nicely browned. Stir in flour. Cook 5 minutes. Add warm stock a little at a time; simmer 30 minutes. If necessary, add a beef bouillon cube to enhance flavor. Swirl in brandy. Spoon soup into ovenproof bowls. Place two slices of bread in each bowl. Top with Swiss cheese. Run under broiler until bubbly and lightly browned. Serves 8.

Brown Stock

2 lb. oxtails

1 lb. bones (veal knuckle, beef shank)

4 tbsp. oil

1 medium onion, chopped

2 carrots, chopped

1 stalk celery, chopped

1 bouquet garni (parsley, bay leaf, thyme)

1 tsp. whole peppercorns

In a stock pot, brown oxtails and bones in oil. Cover with water, about 16 cups. Bring to a boil. Skim brown foam off top. Add onions, carrots, celery, bouquet garni and peppercorns. Bring just to a simmer. Let simmer gently, uncovered; 4 to 5 hours. Strain. Chill overnight. Skim off fat. Return to pan and reduce to half (8 cups).

Not surprisingly, considering its pungency at first raw bite, the onion was for years considered an aphrodisiac—the fate of almost any food that is either expensively rare or takes a bit of getting used to. Preferably, of course, both. Onions (members of the lily family) supply only half that equation, but it was enough to earn them pride of place in one of Pompeii's classiest bordellos in the year 79, Vesuvius's big year . . . to be unearthed there, suffering badly from singe, during excavations some 18 centuries later. Maybe because of this association, onion sellers were not admitted to Pompeii's fruit-and-veg union: social outcasts except at the tradesmen's entrance to the fun palaces, they had to form their own.

WILD MUSHROOM SOUP

Mushroom soup in any form is comfort food indeed.

1 1/2 lb. fresh wild mushrooms, or 8 oz. dried

1 tbsp. olive oil

3 tbsp. butter

1/4 cup finely chopped shallots

2 cloves garlic, finely chopped

2 tbsp. all-purpose flour

5 cups brown stock, heated

1/2 cup 35% cream

Salt and freshly ground pepper

Lemon juice to taste

1 tbsp. finely chopped parsley

Wild mushrooms: Many hitherto exotic varieties (shiitake and oyster mushrooms) are now cultivated and widely available.

Clean, trim and chop mushrooms. (If using dried, cover with warm water and soak 30 minutes. Drain, cut away stem ends, chop; strain soaking liquid and reserve to form part of required stock.) Warm oil and 1 tbsp. butter in a large skillet, and toss mushrooms over medium-high heat for a few minutes. Remove 1 cup mushrooms for use as garnish; keep warm. Add butter to skillet and lightly brown shallots and garlic. Add flour; cook briskly, stirring, 1 to 2 minutes. Whisk in 2 cups of stock. Bring to a boil, lower heat, add remaining stock and simmer 20 minutes. Purée until smooth, and return to saucepan. Swirl in cream, salt, pepper and lemon juice. Ladle soup into warmed bowls. Top with warm reserved mushrooms and sprinkle over parsley. Accompany with homemade crisp toasts. Serves 4.

Tip: Field-type mushrooms may be peeled instead of washed. Remove mushroom stems since they are tough. The stems may be washed, sliced and added to pot when making stock.

Tuscan Vegetable Soup

The secret here is the Parmesan rind—it contributes a wonderfully earthy, musky flavor.

*In my entire life as a cook, I have never spent a day without it on hand.
—Bologna-based cooking maven Marcella Hazan, on Parmesan imperatives.*

1 cup dry white kidney beans
1 bay leaf
Salt
4 cloves garlic, minced
1 1/2 cup onions, chopped
1 tbsp. olive oil
1 cup chopped celery stalks
2 cups chopped carrots
2 cups peeled and cubed potatoes
4 to 6 cups mixed greens (savoy cabbage, kale, spinach, Swiss chard)
1 can (28 oz.) plum tomatoes
1 tsp. dried thyme
1 to 2 small hot red chilies
Freshly ground pepper to taste
1/4 lb. rind of Parmesan cheese

Soak beans in enough water to cover overnight. Drain; place in a large saucepan with 4 cups fresh water and bay leaf. Bring to a boil, reduce heat and simmer 1 hour. Purée half the beans with some cooking liquid, salt and half the garlic; set aside. In a large saucepan, cook onion and remaining garlic in oil 5 minutes. Add celery, carrots, potatoes, greens, tomatoes, thyme, chilies, pepper, remaining whole beans and the cooking liquid, Parmesan rind and about 2 cups water if needed. Bring to boil, reduce heat and simmer, covered, 1 hour. Stir in puréed beans; simmer 30 minutes. Remove rind and bay leaf. Ladle into warm bowls over toasted bread.
Serves 6.

Parmesan Rind: Never discard it until you've cooked with it—in soup, as here, or stews, or risottos, or almost anything that requires thickening or a heady blast of *parmigiano* flavor. Once it's achieved this elutriative consummation, then you must say *addio*, not *arrivederci*.

Before you get to the rind, of course, you will have been the beneficiary of one of the truly exceptional foods—grated or in chunks—of human invention. In the Emilia-Romagna district of north-central Italy some kind of Parmesan has been made for about 2,000 years, and in its present form is some 700 years old.

It is stunningly nutritious. Of all aged cheeses—Parmesan ranges from 18 months to 10 years—*parmigiano-reggiano* (the legal name, stenciled into every wheel-rind) has the highest protein (36%), lowest fat and lowest cholesterol (0.8%) . And yet nearly two gallons of highest-quality cow's milk are concentrated into each pound, and no additives or preservatives are allowed within a thousand country byres. The result is a pure food, easy on wimpy stomachs because of its long aging, stiff with calcium, phosphorus and vitamins A and B_{12} (the great fertilizer for nerve tissue and blood formation, and otherwise found chiefly in fish oil).

America makes its own versions, not aged so long, lacking the original's astounding flavor, but cheaper. Much of this finds its way into mass-market grated Parmesan shakers. Nothing wrong with that; it keeps the price of the shakers down. But this was not the food of Molière, who spent the last years of his life eating little but the genuine article, and writing masterpieces. What cause and effect!

THAI SOUP (TOM KA GAI)

This traditional soup is light and refreshing; suitable as an intro to many styles of main courses. Fish sauce and lime juice are used like salt and pepper in this dish. Create your own balance in taste—and don't let the smell of the fish sauce put you off, you'll never recognize it in the dish.

2 cans (each 14 oz.) coconut milk

3 cups chicken stock

5 kaffir lime leaves

4 stalks lemongrass, white part only, sliced

8 slices fresh ginger, peeled

1 lb. boned chicken breasts, cut in thin strips

2 green onions, thinly sliced

2 tbsp. fish sauce (or to taste)

1/4 cup freshly squeezed lime juice

1 tsp. hot chili paste

1 tbsp. chopped coriander

Whisk coconut milk until smooth. In a large saucepan, combine coconut milk, chicken stock, lime leaves, lemongrass and ginger. Heat through. Simmer gently 10 minutes (do not let boil or coconut milk will separate). Add chicken. Cook over medium heat, stirring occasionally, until done. Add green onions, fish sauce, lime juice, chili paste and coriander. Simmer 5 minutes. Adjust seasonings to taste. Serves 6.

Tip: Soup may be prepared ahead. Reheat very slowly and serve immediately. Do not boil. Chicken stock should be homemade; use the bones from the breast meat and enhance the flavor with bouillon cubes. Use stock flavored with garlic, fresh ginger and green onion. Hot chili paste is a simple way to supply heat. Fresh tiny chilies, thinly sliced, are usually added. If coconut milk should separate, the soup will still taste delicious although it will lose a little in texture and appearance.

LENTIL AND GINGER SOUP

A purée of seasoned lentils makes a superbly restorative soup.

2 tbsp. olive oil

1 small onion, chopped

1 bay leaf

1 tsp. ground ginger

1 slice fresh ginger, peeled

1 tsp. ground cumin

1/2 tsp. dried thyme

1 tsp. ground turmeric

1 cup dried red lentils

2 cups peeled, cubed butternut squash

1 3-inch piece orange rind

4 to 5 cups chicken stock

Salt and freshly ground pepper to taste

1 tbsp. finely chopped parsley

1/4 cup yogurt

In a large heavy pot, cook onion in oil to soften. Add bay leaf, ginger, fresh ginger, cumin, thyme and turmeric; cook briefly. Stir in lentils, squash and orange rind. Add 4 cups chicken stock. Simmer until lentils and squash are cooked through, about 20 minutes. Discard bay leaf, fresh ginger and orange rind. Purée soup until desired consistency. Season with salt and pepper, adding additional stock if desired. Ladle into bowls, sprinkle with parsley and add a spoonful of yogurt.
Serves 6 to 8.

BLACK BEAN SOUP

There are many variations on the theme. Sometimes the beans are mashed to a purée, sometimes there is much liquid, other times almost none. Only one thing is constant—its rib-sticking spicy excellence. In three stages:

One:

1/2 lb. black turtle beans

1/4 lb. pork rind

1 small onion, sliced

2 cloves garlic

6 cups water

1 tsp. salt

Combine black beans, pork rind, onion, garlic and water in a large heavy pot. Bring just to a boil, lower the heat and simmer, covered, until beans are almost tender, about 1 1/2 hours. Stir in salt; stew beans 15 minutes longer.

Two:

2 tbsp. vegetable oil

1/4 lb. bacon, chopped

2 tomatoes, peeled, seeded and chopped

3 serrano chilies or jalapeños, seeded and chopped

2 tbsp. finely chopped Italian parsley

Heat oil in a skillet over moderate heat. Add the rest. Cook over moderate heat for 10 minutes, stirring until nicely thickened.

Three:

Add the tomato mixture to the bean mixture; cook the whole mess together for about 15 minutes more, and some little time later, if your serendipity quotient is high, settle back and enjoy doubly another showing of Blazing Saddles on video.

Serves 6.

Tip: Excellent topped with chopped fresh coriander, a dollop of sour cream, a scattering of shredded Cheddar cheese and chopped onion and tomato.

FISH CHOWDER

ICI ON FAIT LA CHAUDIÈRE: THUS THE SIGNS IN BRETON fishing villages in the nineteenth century. As they had for centuries, fishermen sloshing ashore would save some of their catch for the local innkeeper to use in his ever-simmering cauldron (chaudière) and receive great beakers of the soup in return.

The *chaudière* became anglicized to chowder, crossed the Channel with the Breton sailors to Devon and Cornwall, then the Atlantic to Newfoundland and New England. By the early 1800s it had become so firmly established on the northeast coast that Amelia Simmons, "An American Orphan," whose *American Cookery* was the first English-language cookbook on the continent, gave a full and loving recipe for Boston chowder in her second (1833) edition.

Today, every second one of us has his or her own Boston version, but they all descend from Amelia's, which sounds closer to the Bretons' than ours is, any longer, to hers. The definitive Simmons recipe called for a lining of fatty pork in the bottom of a large pot, then layers of clams (or cod), onions, crumbled hardtack (or sliced potatoes), more fish, more pork, plenty of salt, pepper and garlic and so on up to near the brim. Then add water, or wine, or cider, the author counseled, "until you can just see it," and simmer for 25 minutes. She did not mention milk or cream, which became essentials some 30 years later, and certainly not tomatoes, since many people in her day still believed them to be poisonous.

Any which way, it must have gladdened the human heart as much then as it does now. Here's the *Pequod* crew in Herman Melville's *Moby Dick* (1851), holed up on Nantucket: "Our appetites being sharpened by the frosty voyage, and in particular, Queequeg seeing his favorite fishing food before him, and the chowder being surpassingly excellent, we despatched it with great expedition." Would that all history were so digestible!

The best Boston (New England) chowders these days are made with quahogs (large hard-shelled clams, elsewhere called hard, round or littleneck); make certain, whatever clams you buy, from whichever coast, that their shells are tightly closed. Otherwise you run the risk of being put off chowders and shellfish for life, not to mention life itself.

For other fish chowders, look for firm, lean, light-textured flesh. The fattier species (say, mackerel or eel) add richness, but use in small amounts. Flounders add little flavor, and turn to mush in any prolonged cooking.

In general: *Salt* with care—any amount added must reckon on what is already there. *Herbs, spices*: Choose to suit the base—tarragon, thyme, chervil, chives, bay leaf for a cream; thyme, oregano, basil, bay leaf for a tomato. A touch or two of saffron is good always. Curry, nutmeg, cinnamon, allspice work well if added sparingly. A spoonful or two of *gremolata (p. 27)*, rouille *(p.151)* or aïoli *(p.152)* does wonders for tomato-based chowders.

The one great lesson for mixed chowders is telling the time. Octopus may call for 30 minutes' gentle simmering, a piece of grouper about three, and an oyster no more than a quick dunk in the last unhinging seconds before serving and accepting the plaudits of your own pequodian crew.

FRESHWATER CHOWDER

Verily Canadian, in a country of lakes and rivers teeming with fish.

2 lb. firm white fish fillets (small-mouth bass, pike,
  perch, trout), in chunks

4 cups fish fumet (*recipe on p. 26*)

4 slices bacon, chopped

4 tbsp. butter

1 cup chopped onions

1 cup chopped carrots

1 cup chopped celery

4 cups peeled, diced potatoes

1/2 tsp. thyme

1 bay leaf

1 tsp. salt

2 cups milk

2 cups 10% cream

Chopped parsley for garnish

In a large saucepan, simmer fish gently in fumet about 5 minutes until cooked through. Remove fish with a slotted spoon; set aside. Strain fumet through cheesecloth (a wet Jay cloth works well); reserve. In a heavy pot over medium heat, sauté bacon and onion briefly in butter; toss in carrots and celery, and let stew 5 minutes. Add potatoes to hot fat, toss and cook, about 5 minutes. Stir in reserved fish fumet, thyme, bay leaf and salt. Bring to a simmer, partially cover and cook gently until potatoes are softened, about 20 minutes. Stir in milk, cream and reserved fish; heat through. Discard bay leaf. Ladle into warm bowls, and garnish with parsley.
Serves 8.

Variation: Add fresh corn kernels or 1 or 2 chopped tomatoes just before adding milk.

Basic Fish Fumet

A savory cooking bath for fish or shellfish

2 cups water

2 cups white wine

1 onion, finely chopped

1 carrot, peeled and chopped

1 stalk celery, chopped

1 bay leaf

2 sprigs parsley

2 slices lemon

2 slices fresh ginger

In a medium saucepan, combine all ingredients. Bring just to a boil; simmer 20 minutes. Strain.
Makes about 4 cups, which ought to be enough to do 1 1/2 lb. fish or seafood. Will freeze for no longer than 2 months.

Variation: Use 1 cup dry white vermouth combined with 3 cups water instead of wine and water.

Parmesan Toast

1/2 cup butter, melted or 1/2 cup fruity olive oil

1 clove garlic, minced

1 baguette, cut in 3/4-inch slices

1/2 cup grated Parmesan cheese

Combine butter and garlic. Brush both sides of bread slices with garlic butter and place on baking sheet. Sprinkle with cheese. Bake at 400°F until crispy, about 10 minutes. Run under broiler briefly to brown tops. Makes approximately 14.

CIOPPINO

Not officially a chowder, but one of the great fish stews.

2 cloves garlic, chopped

1 red onion, chopped

6 tbsp. fruity olive oil

1 can (28 oz.) plum tomatoes, drained and chopped

1 bay leaf

1/2 tsp. dried oregano

1/2 tsp. dried basil

1 cup white wine

1 cup Basic Fish Fumet (*recipe on p. 26*)

24 clams (or mussels), scrubbed, soaked in cold water
   20 minutes and rinsed

1 lb. shrimp, unpeeled

1 lb. firm, white fish fillets, cut in large chunks

2 crab legs, in serving pieces

Salt and freshly ground pepper

1 tbsp. finely chopped parsley for garnish

Parmesan Toast (*recipe on p. 26*) **or crusty bread**

Gremolata: Combine 1 tbsp. each grated lemon rind, grated Parmesan, finely chopped parsley and minced garlic. Perfect agent for tomato-based soups and stews.

In a large heavy pot over medium heat, soften garlic and onions in oil. Add tomatoes, cooking briskly to thicken. Stir in bay leaf, oregano, basil and wine, reducing about 2 minutes. Gradually stir in fumet, and bring just to a simmer. Toss in clams and cook, covered, 5 minutes; add shrimp, and simmer another 5 minutes; repeat with fish, then crab. Season to taste. Discard bay leaf and any unopened clams. Spoon into large bowls and garnish with parsley, Serve with Parmesan Toasts. Freshly grated Parmesan cheese or gremolata make a nice finish. Serves 6.

Tip: Tomatoes are one of the most seasonal of vegetables. Since a truly ripe, flavorful tomato is a rare thing indeed, it's best to use canned tomatoes when fresh are not in season. Our preference is to use plum tomatoes. Experiment to find the brand you like the best.

Small Dishes

CHICKEN WINGS

I T'S HARD TO CREDIT, BUT THE CHICKEN WING AS WE KNOW it is only about 30 years old. Even today the wing (as we know it) is unknown in much of Europe. A friend from Italy, on his first visit to these shores last year, surveyed a dish of barbecued flats and drumettes and concluded it was a joke. "*E un scherzo, claro*," he suggested hesitantly. "Legs from a very small chicken, no?" No, *wings*. He shook his head, plainly longing to be back in the land of veal, where things were the proper size.

By fixing the wing's birth in 1964, no disrespect is meant to Chinese or African Americans, both of whom have relished it for centuries. By "wing as we know it" we mean the version now seen, in maximized profusion, at every bar on the continent. This wing's birth can be traced to the year and the place, because *The New Yorker's* Calvin Trillin did the tracing. After wide and diligent research, Trillin concluded that the wing that started it all really did originate in Buffalo, New York—specifically in Frank and Teressa Bellissimo's Anchor Bar on Main Street.

Exactly how the invention sprang from the Bellissimos' brows is not clear, but all agree on the year, as well as the peppery sauce, the celery and the cooling blue cheese dressing that helped make their wings—*Buffalo* wings—a bar-grazing hit far beyond their city's borders. Today we eat them from Nome to Key Largo, Bakersfield to Bonavista: so eclectic and far-flung is their success that one wonders why the Buffalo city parents have not yet taken up the suggestion to name a sports team the Buffalo Wings. It would carry more locational freight than Bills or Sabres.

However we cook or eat wings among consenting adults at home, we owe Teressa Bellissimo full credit for the way she prepared hers. The raw wing is an ungainly sight, something a skinned bat might look like.

Mrs. Bellissimo smartly cut off the wing tip, which was about as useful as a seventh toe, then chopped the wing in half—separating the flat portion, with the succulent meat between the two thin bones, from the miniature drumstick, then and thereafter called the drumette. This eminently simple stroke of brilliance makes a bunch of prepared wings look like an ordinary plate of chicken parts seen through the wrong end of a telescope; our Italian friend's conclusion was wrong but reasonable. It also makes them easier to cook and tidier to eat.

Wing tips:

Count on at least four wings (eight pieces) per person, though many demand double that even to start; 2 1/2 lb. means about 16 wings, for four people. Then do like Mrs. Bellissimo: sever and discard the wing tip and cut through at the joint of next two sections. Result: one flat, one drumette. Pat dry.

To broil: Cover bottom of pan with foil; broil on rack 5 inches from heat, about 7 minutes per side, basting twice.

To barbecue: Cook 5 inches from heat about 20 minutes, basting and turning until your wrist aches.

To deep-fry: Cook in oil (peanut or shortening) at 350°F, a few at a time, 4 to 5 minutes, until crisply golden.

To bake: Wings take on a different dimension if marinated and then baked at 350°F in the marinade. Cover for the first 20 minutes, then uncover and bake another 20 to 30 minutes.

Many like their wings straight, or straightish: hold the diversions, just let us at them. Others grow wild-eyed and distraught if deprived of something to dip into, as if they have been somehow cheated. They suggest, no matter the succulently moist evidence in their fingers, that without a dip every single wing will be hopelessly and irretrievably dry.

BUFFALO CHICKEN WINGS

The ultimate Buffalo chicken wing, in our experience, is found a few miles south, at the Silver Fox in Ellicottville, N.Y., a great little town that comes alive during the skiing season. The secret to these is Frank's sauce of aged and blended hot peppers, and if you don't know what that is it's time you learned; the alchemy is waiting for you at the supermarket. Here's our version.

16 chicken wings
Oil for deep-frying
1/4 cup melted butter
2 tbsp. Frank's Red Hot Sauce, or more

Cut tips from chicken wings. Sever at the joint. Dry well. Deep-fry at 350°F until golden brown and crisp. Melt butter and hot sauce in a small pot. In a plastic container with a lid, toss eight or so wings at a time, with 2 tbsp. of the sauce. Keep warm in oven until all are cooked, then serve with Blue Cheese Dressing (recipe follows). Should serve 4, but 2 may be more like it.

Blue Cheese Dressing
1/2 cup mayonnaise
1/4 cup sour cream
1/4 lb. blue cheese, crumbled

Blend mayo and sour cream with half the cheese until smooth. Stir in remaining cheese.

THAI WINGS

We learned these from a great professional cook, Linda Stephens, of Toronto, who learned them in Bangkok.

16 chicken wings, tips removed, severed at joint

4 cloves garlic, minced

2 tbsp. grated fresh ginger

1 stalk lemongrass, sliced

4 green onions, chopped

1/4 cup lime juice

2 tsp. grated lime rind

1/3 cup hoisin sauce

2 tbsp. fish sauce

2 tbsp. soy sauce

1 tbsp. hot chili paste

1/4 cup honey

Chopped fresh mint or coriander

With a sharp knife, scrape down meat and skin of each wing's middle section to form a nub at the joint; remove as well the smaller bone, leaving only one to serve as drumstick. Mint excepting, combine remaining ingredients in a bowl, coat wings and marinate overnight in refrigerator. Bake on a greased foil-lined pan at 400°F for 30 minutes, then broil to crispen skin. Serve hot or cold. Garnish with mint. Serves 4.

TEX-MEX

THE MEXICAN INFLUENCE HAS BEEN PUSHING ACQUISI-
tively northward for at least two decades. But its
traditions, so imbedded in Texas, Arizona and New
Mexico—followed by California and to a growing
extent by Colorado, which would be California if it could—
are still relatively new discoveries upward and inland from
the 32nd parallel. Fast-food outlets are the great bellwethers
and proselytizers. They wouldn't exist if there was no demand,
but their standardized, assembly-line brand of Tex-Mex tub-
thumping too often proves to be a god that failed.

The principal culprit, as always with assembly lines, is
impersonality. Border cooking tends to be simple stuff, nothing insanely sophisto, but deceptive all the same. We might
remember that it is the descendant of pre-Columbian
kitchens, our inheritance from the Maya, the Toltecs, the
Aztecs, who an eon or two ago domesticated the turkey, gave
the world the tomato and transformed a plant that began as
wild grass into what we now know as sweet corn; a heritage
not to be taken for granted. This is hands-on, *personal* food,
requiring skill to arrive at just the right balance of ingredients, spices, color. Patience and experimentation are key.

To this end the patient experimenter should have in
the larder such matters as blue corn flour, blue cornmeal,
fresh coriander, *jicama* (white, turniplike flavor), pinto beans,
corn husks, pine nuts, Mexican chocolate (drier and more
bitter than we're used to), tomatillos (no kin to the tomato;
they have a lemony bite), *nopales* (juicy cactus pads available
mostly in jars: if you can find them fresh, carefully remove
the ferocious spines, boil till tender and slice), chilies (fresh
and dried) and, above all, chili powder.

Chilies: They originated in South America, not the Orient, as many suppose (though India gave us the peppercorn, which is unrelated). Growers measure their comparative heat in something called Scoville units, after Wilbur Scoville, who devised the scale in 1912. Bell and pimiento peppers start, naturally, at zero; the hot variety ranges from anaheim (250 to 1,500 Scoville units) through the medium poblanos and pasillas (about 3,000) to the fiery jalapeños, long greens and serranos (4,000 to 25,000). In eastern North America, "jalapeño" has become lazy shorthand for hot peppers as a whole, "the all-American hot pepper," as Amal Naj, a leading authority on peppers, calls it. He points out that nearly 90 percent of jalapeños in the northern continent are imported from Mexico, where chilies have been grown for at least 9,000 years.

The habañero pepper, much loved by the Maya (who sneer at jalapeños), is walnut-shaped, packs some 300,000 Scoville units, or 15 times the heat of a jalapeño, and is the hottest readily available pepper on earth. So hot, Amal Naj reports, that a Texan recently looked into the possibilities of using it for tear gas.

For the truly fetishistic heat fanatic, content with nothing but the absolute, there is the rare rocoto (*Capsicum pubescens*), which some who have risked it say is even hotter than the habañero. Also known as *chile caballo* and *chile perón*, it is grown mainly in the Peruvian Andes and in small areas of Honduras, Guatemala and Mexico; it takes a long time distilling its fury and needs about a dozen hours of daily sunlight, which rules out its cultivation any farther north. Peruvians call it, locally, *gringo huanuchi*, gringo killer, and *levanta muertos*, raise the dead. The former is the kind of joke that will goad the heat-besotted north of the Rio Grande to seek it out and prove the Peruvians wrong. The latter is what they can hope for when they prove the Peruvians right.

Whichever you choose, use with caution and economy. Remember that the source of the heat is in the seeds: to reduce heat, reduce the seeds. And when one day you scald your buds—and you will—be kind: water or beer are no help. Honey, sugar and yogurt are better extinguishers by far.

Fajitas

Derived from *faja*, Spanish for girdle, with a dimunitive suffix. After fajitas crossed the Mexican border into Texas, they were tenderized in the open arms of soft warm tortillas. If using beef, sirloin is best—but flank steak will do.

1 tbsp. paprika

1 tbsp. dried oregano

1 tsp. celery seed

1 tbsp. dried thyme

1 tbsp. cumin

2 tbsp. chili powder

1 tbsp. ground cinnamon

2 tbsp. tomato paste

4 tbsp. lemon juice

1/4 cup olive oil

2 cloves garlic, minced

1 small onion, finely chopped

1 large onion, thinly sliced

2 peppers (red, yellow or green), seeded and thinly sliced

4 tbsp. olive oil

2 lbs. pork or lamb tenderloin or boneless chicken breasts

Warming tortillas: Wrap 2 tortillas in plastic wrap, microwave on medium 30 seconds or wrap 4 tortillas in tinfoil, heat in 350°F oven for 5 minutes or heat in foil on the barbecue.

Combine spices, herbs, tomato paste, lemon juice, 1/4 cup olive oil, garlic and minced onion to make a thick paste. Slice tenderloins in thin strips and add to marinade. Let stand overnight. Remove from marinade. Barbecue or fry until just cooked through. Fry onions and peppers in olive oil until nicely browned. Serve meat or chicken in warm tortillas topped with sautéed onion and choice of sour cream, Guacamole (p. 37), Salsa Cruda (p. 36), and/or grated cheddar cheese.

Serves 4.

SALSA CRUDA

1 to 2 jalapeño chilies, seeded and finely chopped

2 cups tomatoes, seeded and finely chopped

4 garlic cloves, minced

1 small onion, finely chopped

2 tbsp. finely chopped coriander

2 tbsp. lime or lemon juice

Salt and freshly ground pepper

Pebre

This sauce is served throughout Chile. Prepare as salsa but mince ingredients finely. Use 2 small chilies in place of jalapeño and 1/2 cup water. Let stand 2 to 3 hours.

Toss it all together, mix well, let stand. Makes 3 cups. The essentials are tomatoes and onions, but excellent additional variants are sweet peppers, avocado and/or cooked corn. At your preference, add 1 cup of any such to the above. A cinch to make, cheap as the dawn, additive-free, thoroughly good for you: no wonder commercial salsa sales have leapfrogged past ketchup. And that's not counting the ones you make.

Tip: To intensify the flavors, set tomatoes and chilies on the barbecue or in a very hot oven and cook until skins are well charred.

GUACAMOLE

This is a delicate foil for spicy foods, but it's marvellous any time.

1 small onion, chopped

2 serrano chilies or 1 jalapeño chile seeded and finely chopped

1 clove garlic, chopped

2 tbsp. coriander, chopped

2 tbsp. fresh lime juice

2 avocados

2 medium tomatoes, seeded and chopped

Salt to taste

Mash together half the onion and 1 tbsp. coriander with the garlic and chilies to make a paste. Halve the avocados, remove the pits and scoop out the flesh. Mash one avocado with the chili paste (a potato masher does a good job). Chop the other. Combine avocado, onion, tomato, coriander and lime juice. Do not over blend: the dip should have some texture. Serve pronto. (If this is not possible, preserve the freshness and flavor by sticking the avocado pit in the middle of the guacamole and store in an airtight container in the fridge.)

Makes 2 cups

Tip: Spread top of guacamole with a thin layer of sour cream. Cover the whole lot with plastic wrap. Refrigerate. Stir before serving.

TEX-MEX CHILI

Traditional Tex-Mex cooks chop their own beef rather than buying it ground. Start with well-trimmed stewing beef or, for a different flavor, replace part of the beef with pork or spicy sausage. (Pictured opposite page 56.)

10 dried ancho chilies

4 dried chipotle chilies

2 to 4 fresh or canned jalapeños

4 tbsp. lard, bacon fat or oil

4 medium onions, chopped

2 tbsp. finely chopped garlic

3 lb. stewing beef, finely chopped

1 tbsp. each paprika and ground cumin

1 tsp. each dried oregano and basil

2 cups fresh tomatoes, peeled, seeded and chopped (or equivalent canned)

2 to 4 cups beef stock or water

Salt and freshly ground black pepper

3 cups cooked red kidney beans or pinto beans

Prepare a purée from the ancho and chipotle chilies. Boil, peel, seed and chop fresh jalapeños (or rinse and chop canned ones). Set aside. In a heavy skillet, heat 2 tbsp. fat over medium heat. Add onions; cook until soft. Stir in garlic; cook for a few minutes. Set aside. In a large, heavy saucepan, heat remaining fat. Add beef and brown lightly, in batches if necessary. Add cooked onions and garlic, chili purée, paprika, cumin, oregano and basil; toss briefly. Stir in tomatoes, stock, salt and pepper. Bring to a boil, lower heat and simmer, partially covered, for 1 1/2 to 2 hours, stirring occasionally. Before serving, taste and adjust seasoning; stir in jalapeños and beans, or serve them alongside. Garnish with all manner of good stuff: sour cream, shredded Cheddar cheese, chopped tomato.
Serves 6 to 8.

GOAT CHEESE

I T'S A TOSS-UP WHETHER THE GOAT OR THE DOG WAS THE first animal to be domesticated some 9,000 years ago. Certainly the goat has been the more productive for human needs: from the earliest days it has supplied milk, meat and wool (mohair and cashmere), later adding kid gloves and cheese to its product line.

And what has the goat to show for its pains? One way or another it has lent its name—courtesy the domesticators—to bloody-mindedness, playing the fool, being the fall guy and to ludicrously horny behavior among retired males.

It deserves better, not least because it deserves respect. Check out the eyes. They are remarkable. No-nonsense, level-gazed, inclined to humor, they bespeak an intelligence rare in ruminants. Just compare a goat's eyes with a cow's vacant watery ones, which give special meaning to the word *bovine*, or to the shallow, shifty looks of the sheep, the goat's close cousin in genealogy but remotely distant in independence, vigor and all-round smarts. In herd-world sociology, it's the difference between speed-readers and lip-movers.

This is not simple prejudice. Anyone who has been around goats will agree. They like space, they abhor being cooped up. If they are, they'll do their damnedest to find a way out: once one finds it, the finder teaches the others. They are fastidiously neat and clean, and they plainly get a kick out of life: not for nothing does *caper*, as in frolic, come from the Latin word for the goat genus. Texans run them with their flocks of merino sheep, since the goats selflessly eat the thorns and thistles that would otherwise ruin the expensive merino wool. (Everything has its price, of course: later, as a kind of kid pro quo, "Judas goats" lead their cousins to the slaughterhouse.)

Goat products have an unquestionably stronger taste than our more usual dairy foods. In fact, goat's milk, served ice cold, is refreshingly delicious and more easily digestible (having smaller fat globules) than cow's, and its meat, when young, tender as a lamb's but with a richer flavor, can be one of the great delicacies. As for goat cheese, for years it had social acceptance on a par with head cheese: the same people sniffed at it—altogether too *pungent*, reeking of things better left unsaid—who thought nothing of buying the rankest Stilton or room-clearing Limburger by the kilo.

The turnaround came in the mid-eighties, by which time even the sniffers realized that goat cheese is not only light (as low as 15% butterfat) but memorable (nutty, tart, peppery), and not only memorable but rare (a doe rarely produces more than three quarts of milk a day, compared with a cow's profligate 20 or so). All that remained was to get rid of *goat cheese*. Bypass *feta*, which was somehow stuck with Greek salads, look up the French, as always when in doubt, and presto! *chèvre*. Haute goat.

The first North American commercial goat-cheese producers were in Quebec (1979)—the Benedictine nuns of Joliette, and René Marceau and Lucie Chartrier of La Ferme Tournevent in Chesterville. In 1990, Laura Chenel of Sonoma County, California, who was among the first to produce it in the United States, gave it priceless publicity with *Chèvre: The Goat Cheese Cookbook*, the sort of seminal work that begins, "Making goat cheese is amazingly simple," then continues, with daunting attention to the finest details, to prove it is anything but unless your name is Laura Chenel.

Aside from salads, goat cheese is an excellent "cooker." Some suggestions:

• Fresh young cheese should be eaten within days; cover in plastic wrap. A cheese to be aged should be lightly wrapped in foil and kept in the fridge's butter compartment.

A case in point: Crottin de Chavignol, which is at the richest and most redolent end of the goat ledger (a fact proudly underlined by its name, meaning Chavignol dung).

    • For a memorable fast sandwich, top a slice of whole wheat toast with some sliced ham and crumbled goat cheese; broil briefly.

    • For breakfast, tuck it into an omelette or stir into scrambled eggs.

    • For potatoes, use instead of sour cream on baked ones; add chives. Stir into mashed ones with butter, parsley, minced celeriac.

    • Remember that gentle heat (as with all cheeses) is best; that the goat's robust and quickening flavors are complemented best by the concomitant flavors of the Mediterranean. And awhey we go.

HERBED GOAT CHEESE

Spread on pumpernickel, crumble into lightly dressed greens, or bake slices at 350°F a few minutes and serve warm over greens.

1 cup extra virgin olive oil

2 cloves garlic, sliced

2 bay leaves

2 to 3 sprigs fresh thyme

2 small sprigs fresh rosemary

1 tbsp. mixed white, black, green peppercorns

1 tsp. pink peppercorns

8 small rounds firm goat cheese

Heat oil gently until surface shimmers. Pour onto garlic, herbs, peppercorns; cool. Place cheese in single layer in a shallow glass dish; pour over oil. Refrigerate, covered, 24 hours. Use at room temperature. Serves 8.

WARM GOAT CHEESE SALAD

Tangy salad leaves (arugula, endive, radicchio and lamb's lettuce)
4 slices soft goat cheese, about 1/2 inch thick
Fruity olive oil
1/4 cup walnuts, toasted
Walnut Dressing (*recipe follows*)
Parmesan Toast (*recipe on p. 26*)

Wash, dry and trim leaves; chill. Brush cheese with a little oil. Place on an oiled baking sheet. Warm at 350°F for 5 to 8 minutes, until cheese is just melting and beginning to brown. Quickly toss leaves and nuts in Walnut Dressing, and arrange on four plates. Top each with melted cheese, and accompany with warm Parmesan Toast and lots of freshly ground pepper.
Serves 4.

Walnut Dressing
2 tbsp. sherry vinegar
2 tsp. Dijon mustard
1/2 cup walnut oil
Salt and freshly ground pepper to taste

Combine all ingredients well.

Variation: Use Herbed Goat Cheese (*p. 41*).

OLIVES

NATURE HAS ORDAINED THAT EVERYTHING THE OLIVE gives is beautiful: the tree, the color, the wood, the fruit (with a bit of help from sinful man) and above all, the oil, one of the great healthful boons to the thinking cook.

Consider its history. Ancient peoples fell over themselves claiming the olive's invention: the Egyptians may have staked their claim first, 6,000 years ago, on behalf of their great goddess Isis. Grateful Greeks claimed much the same thing when they named their capital after the goddess Athena, who struck the ground with her spear and gave them the olive tree that resulted. Ancient Rome regarded it as every bit as sacred to the goddess Minerva. Noah, in Old Testament timelessness, knew the Flood was over when the dove dropped by the ark with an olive branch in its mouth.

And its uses. The fruit as food; the oil as medicine, as cooking agent, as soap and perfume; the wood as building agent for the ages. The Egyptians used it as a lubricant to help move the monstrous blocks of stone that formed the pyramids; the Romans as a fuel for their lamps, as a medicine for almost anything that ailed them, as a food preservative for fish (so still used today, of course), as grease for chariot axles, as weed killer, as insect inhibitor; the Israelites used the wood for the tabernacle of Solomon's Temple. It has indelibly marked the cooking, as we enjoy it now, of the Middle East, Greece, Portugal, Spain, southern France and Italy (where it became widespread in the north, curiously, only after World War II). Roman Catholics use it to anoint babies, bishops and the dying, certainly a catholic reach. The Church of England used it to anoint Queen Elizabeth II at her coronation. And Epicure uses it like crazy ourselves.

What distinguishes the olive above all is Character. It's there in the trees, gnarled and stupendously weathered

If I could paint and had the necessary time, I should devote myself for a few years to making pictures only of olive trees. What a wealth of variations upon a single theme.
—Aldous Huxley

by centuries (they think nothing of living for 600 years and more, so long as frost doesn't cut them off in the prime of their youth), yet always profusely producing fruit from their generous branches. It's there in the wood, close-grained, slow-growing, hard as truth. It's there in the fruit, which does not easily yield its pleasures but must be pickled, cured or washed long in water to be made edible: uncured, a glucoside called oleuropein makes the freshly picked olive unbearably bitter, whether unripe green or fully ripe black-purple. It's there in the oil, magnificent end product that adds both taste and nutrition to any dish lucky enough to be so blessed.

Marinate green olives in your favorite martini mix. Tanqueray with a splash, dash and a sprinkle of dry vermouth. Leave for a few hours or overnight. Outstanding.

Nutrition, yes. There was a time there, starting in the suddenly sanctimonious seventies, when olives and their oil were looked at askance by the nutritional great and good. Saturate-wise, it was neutral—a monounsaturate in a climate that touted polyunsaturates such as safflower as the new frontlines in the war against artery-silting cholesterol.

Yet, no matter what their cholesterol levels, people can still think. And they started wondering: how come Mediterranean people, the inheritors of Isis, of Athena, of Minerva—yea, even of Noah—seemed to live just as long as we do, and in the main look a whole lot happier doing so?

It was the Great Mediterranean Conundrum, and one of the first to address it was a friend of ours who in 1964 made a documentary film for American TV about the little town of Roseto, Pennsylvania. Why Roseto? the film asked. How come this small burg (pop. then about 1,300) could have about the highest cholesterol diet per capita in the U.S.—and one of its lowest rates of heart disease? They had to be doing something right.

Thirty years later, armed with accumulating studies from dietary think tanks, we can figure that Rosetans—southern Italian immigrants almost to a man, woman and child—could thank their wholesale ingestion of olive oil. (And doubtless red wine, too, since many authorities now include

*The whole
Mediterranean, the
sculpture, the palms,
the gold beads, the
bearded heroes, the
wine, the ideas, the
ships, the moonlight,
the winged gorgons,
the bronze men, the
philosophers
—all of it seems to
rise in the sour,
pungent taste of
these black olives
between the teeth.
A taste older than
meat, older than
wine. A taste as
old as cold water.
—Lawrence Durrell,
1945.*

its beneficial effects as part of the Mediterranean equation.) A typical latter-day report in *Medical World News* noted that coronary heart disease in men between 55 and 65 is 10 times higher in the United States than, for example, in Greece, the number-two olive producer in the world (after Spain, thanks to the olive-loving Moors).

So the Romans were right in believing the olive to be good medicine: among other things, it contains salicylic acid, the active ingredient in aspirin. As the olive has grown in favor, the polyunsaturates have been losing ground. Scientists now say that the polys lower our *good* cholesterol (high-density lipoproteins) as well as our bad (the low-density lips), whereas olive oil, the mighty mono, lowers the LDLs and raises the HDLs at the same time. No tears in this corner for the polys: the oil of the olive adds distinction and flavor wherever it is used, drenching us in sun, but who knows what safflower oil tastes or smells like?

Besides, the very word *oil* derives from the ancient Greek for olive. Every time we use it, in whatever context, from whatever source, safflower or diesel, we pay homage to the great progenitor. To Isis, perhaps.

CYPRUS-STYLE MARINATED OLIVES

2 tsp. coriander seeds

2 cups firm green olives, rinsed, drained, pitted and finely chopped

1/4 cup extra virgin olive oil

1/4 cup red wine vinegar

2 large cloves garlic, minced

Lightly roast coriander seeds, then crush with mortar and pestle (or whirl in a spice mill). In a bowl, combine with remaining ingredients. Refrigerate, covered, for at least 1 hour. Serve with bread.
Makes 2 cups.

It's advisable to taste olives before you buy to judge whether the texture and flavor are what you want. Labeling can be misleading. The most frequently available varieties are as follows.

FROM ITALY:
Gaeta: mild, black, dry-salt cured or brine cured.
Ligurian: tasty, black-brown, salt-brine cured.
Bella Di Ceriguola: a rare and pricey monster green olive with a curious avocado-like flavor, from a small estate in Italy's Southern Puglia region. For those who insist, against widespread martini dogma, that the olive at the bottom should be consumed as the climax rather than shunned as the anti.
Taggiasca: also from Liguria, the best pitted olive available; brown-black, flavorful, packed in oil and herbs.

FROM GREECE:
Kalamata: purple-black, slit, then brine cured.
Royal: reddish dark brown or light brown; slit, then brine cured and packed with vinegar and olive oil.
Cracked green: cracked and salt-brine cured. Crisp, clean flavor.

FROM MOROCCO:
Black, wrinkled, dry-salt cured, meaty. Rub with oil, garlic and spices.

FROM FRANCE:
Nyons: black with greenish tinge, dry-salt cured, then rubbed with oil-packed with stems and leaves.
Picholine: smallish smooth green olive, salt-brine cured, distinctive mild flavor.
Niçoise: dark brown, salt-brine cured, small with large pit. Sometimes packed with oils and herbs.

FROM SPAIN:
Spanish-style: bright green, of various sizes, and with various stuffings; lye cured, then packed in salt and acid brine.

Tip: Keep your olives in a cool place in a covered jar. If you plan to keep them for more than a day or two, cover them with brine (either the brine they came with or make your own) or cover with oil.

TAPENADE

The luxury version of a simple classic.

1 cup pitted black olives (ligurian preferably)
2 tbsp. chopped sun-dried tomatoes in oil
2 anchovies, chopped
1 clove garlic, minced
2 tbsp. finely diced onion
1/4 cup chopped parsley
1/4 cup fruity olive oil
1 tbsp. freshly squeezed lemon juice

Combine olives, sun-dried tomatoes, anchovies, garlic and onion in blender. Process to finely chop. Add remaining ingredients. Blend briefly just to mix. Let stand for 1 hour or more to allow flavors to meld. Serve on little toasts or with a crusty baguette.
Makes 1 cup.

Tip: Toss tapenade with warm rotini for an interesting pasta sauce. Add fresh basil and a sliced roasted red or yellow pepper.

Sun-dried Tomatoes: Look for bright orangy color and soft texture, intensely flavored. Plump up by steaming for 10 minutes. A good bet is to buy those sold in jars with top-quality olive oil. Drain well before using.

TAPENADE MINIPIZZAS

Pizza dough (*recipe follows*)
Tapenade (*recipe above*)
1 1/2 cups shredded mozzarella cheese
Light olive oil
Whole ripe olives
Grated lemon rind,
Finely chopped fresh thyme or parsley

Divide pizza dough into 16 portions, and on a lightly floured surface, roll into 4-inch rounds. Place minipizzas on unglazed ceramic tiles— best for a crisp bottom crust—or on a sturdy baking sheet. Spread some tapenade on each round. Top with mozzarella and a few drops of olive oil. Bake at 400°F about 10 or 12 minutes, until crust is cooked and minipizzas are lightly browned. Top each with an olive tossed in oil, a little lemon rind and fresh herbs.

Variation: Top with tapenade, sliced sundried tomatoes (in oil) and fresh rosemary. Or try with tapenade, chunks of goat cheese, and sliced olives and fresh rosemary.

Meze

Not strictly appetizers, these nibbles can appear with drinks at any time of day. The idea is to combine colors, aromas, flavors; fresh or pickled vegetables; nuts; meat patties; savory tartlets; peppered figs; olives; small fried or smoked fish; octopus; feta.

Pizza Dough

2 to 2 1/2 cups all-purpose flour

2 tsp. sugar

1 tsp. salt

1 tbsp. fast-acting dry yeast

1 cup very warm water

1/4 cup olive oil

In a large bowl, mix 1 cup flour with sugar, salt and yeast. Combine water and oil; add to dry ingredients, beating until smooth. Gradually stir in enough remaining flour to make a soft dough. Knead on a floured surface for a few minutes. Form dough into a ball, place in a greased bowl and turn so that all the dough is greased. Cover with a damp cloth and let stand in a warm place until doubled in bulk. Punch down. Roll or pat dough into two 12-inch circles about 1/8 inch thick. Place on lightly oiled pizza tins or baking sheets—for the best crispy crust, place on preheated unglazed ceramic tiles. Pinch edges up to form a small rim. Spread with your favorite toppings. Drizzle olive oil on top and bake at 400°F for about 20 minutes or until crust is lightly browned and topping sizzles.
Makes 2 12-inch pizzas or 16 4-inch appetizer pizzas.

ROAST PEPPER BRUSCHETTA

Bruschetta has become generic for almost anything found on top of bread. This version is so filling that one or two slices per person before dinner are more than sufficient.

2 sweet red peppers, roasted and peeled

2 sweet yellow peppers, roasted and peeled

1 clove garlic, minced

1/4 cup finely minced red onion

2 tbsp. finely minced sun-dried tomatoes (optional)

1 tsp. balsamic vinegar or 1 tbsp. lemon juice

2 tbsp. finely chopped parsley

1 tbsp. finely chopped fresh basil

Olive oil to taste

Salt and freshly ground pepper to taste

1 bread stick (Calabrese)

2 cloves garlic, halved

2 cups shredded mozzarella cheese

2 tbsp. grated Parmesan cheese

Finely chop roasted peppers. Combine with minced garlic, onion tomatoes (if using), vinegar, parsley, basil, olive oil, salt and pepper. Slice bread diagonally in 3/4-inch slices. Brush liberally with olive oil. Bake at 400°F for 5 minutes or until lightly browned, turning once. Rub toast with halved garlic cloves. Top with mozzarella. Return to oven for 2 minutes. Spoon pepper mixture on top and sprinkle with Parmesan cheese. Return to oven until bubbly, about 2 minutes. Makes 14 to 16.

Tip: This basic mixture is superb on pizza (especially topped with goat cheese). Serve on top of grilled chicken breast or grilled fish. Or serve on Parmesan Toast (p. 26)

Tip: Peppers may be halved or quartered, seeded, brushed with olive oil and grilled on the barbecue or in a very hot oven. Makes a great vegetable dish or, thinly sliced, an excellent addition to vegetable salads.

Roasted Peppers: Broil whole peppers over coals until skins char and blister. (May also be done in a very hot oven; 450°F for 15 minutes. Set on baking tray lined with tinfoil.) Place in a bowl and cover with plastic wrap. Let cool. Skins will slip off easily. Seed and slice.

Bocconcini and Sun-Dried Tomatoes in Olive Oil

Bocconcini: Originally made in Italy from the milk of buffalo, but hard to find today and impossible to import. What's sold in North America are small fresh mozzarella cheeses made domestically from pasteurized cow's milk. Rinse daily with cold water. Keep covered with fresh water while in the refrigerator, but not for long.

What restaurants should use more often when local fully ripe tomatoes aren't available.

8 bocconcini, sliced (2 cups)

1/4 cup sun-dried tomatoes (in oil), slivered

16 ripe niçoise or ligurian olives, halved, pitted

2 tbsp. coarsely chopped Italian parsley

2 tbsp. coarsely chopped fresh basil

3 tbsp. extra virgin olive oil

Freshly cracked black pepper

Toss bocconcini, tomatoes, olives and herbs in oil; then pepper.
Marinate 30 minutes.
Serves 4 as part of an antipasto plate.

Olive Oil

The familiar denominations of grade, from extra virgin at the top to refined table oil at the bottom, ostensibly imply preparation methods (extra virgin from the first cold pressings of the fruits, and so on), but European regulations that enforce the denominations measure only the level of acidity.

The best oils come from small estates (notably robust ones coming from Portugal and Spain) that do their own processing. Use simply: for instance, drizzle over carpaccio, fresh fish or grilled vegetables with nothing else except ground pepper.

For all-round usage make sure to find a good blend made by a reliable producer. Let your palate be the guide.

FOCACCIA WITH OLIVES AND ROSEMARY

A food processor reduces the labor, but the texture will be a little finer if ingredients are mixed by hand. An accompaniment to soups, salads and cheeses; or slice horizontally and make a special sandwich.

1 1/2 tbsp. fast-acting active dry yeast

3/4 cup warm water

1 1/2 cups unbleached all-purpose flour

1 to 2 tbsp. olive oil, and extra

1/2 cup pitted ripe olives, quartered

Several small sprigs rosemary

Kosher or sea salt

Marinated Olives

Combine 1 cup each ripe and green olives, 4 halved garlic cloves, 1 tsp. rosemary, slivered rind of 1 lemon, 2 tbsp. lemon juice and enough olive oil to cover. Enjoy the olives with drinks or on their own. Use the leftover marinade to baste or marinade meat or vegetables for the grill.

Dissolve yeast in 1/4 cup water; stir in 2 tbsp. flour. Set aside, covered with a damp cloth, until double in size. Place remaining flour in bowl of food processor with steel blade attached; add yeast mixture, 1 tbsp. oil and remaining water; whirl briefly. Add 1/4 cup olives; whirl again until mixture forms a ball (or hand mix in a large bowl). Set aside. Turn dough out onto a floured surface, cover, let stand and knead until smooth. Form into a ball, and set in a bowl. Cover and let stand in a warm place until double in size. Punch down, and knead again briefly. On a floured surface and using a floured rolling pin, roll into a circle 3/4 inch thick. Place on an oiled baking sheet and dimple top with fingertips. Decorate with remaining olives and rosemary. Brush with some oil and scatter with salt. Allow to rise again, about 30 minutes. Bake at 375°F for 30 minutes or until cooked and lightly browned.

Variation: Add crumbled goat cheese to topping with olives and herbs. Omit olives from dough.

Vegetables and Salads

W E HAVE ALWAYS KNOWN VEGETABLES ARE GOOD FOR us, since mother told us For The Last Time to finish them up or we wouldn't get out to play with Jimmy before bedtime, or indeed ever again. What we increasingly know is just how good they are, and that we ignore them—or ignore cooking them with decent attention—at our peril.

For starters, vegetables are low in calories. Since reducing caloric intake alone is one of the simplest ways of reducing the incidence of cancer, it follows that the more veggies we eat, the better for us: we will simply have less room for animal fats. A kind of negative plus.

Naturally, there's more to it than that, and it has to do with some notably nasty molecules we're learning to call free radicals. This is a deceptively benign name (in the sixties it would have been a call to the barricades and Norman Mailer would have written white-hot books about them) for particles that, unchecked, mutate genes and form the basis for cancer. Our bodies make them while converting energy and using oxygen, and we manage to mop up most of them with our own protective anti-oxidant enzymes. What vegetables provide in abundance—particularly the yellows and greens, the roots and the leafy ones, the cabbages, the broccolis, the Brussels sprouts—are more of those compounds, including vitamins E and C, and beta carotene, which converts into vitamin A in the body.

The good news is that we're eating more of the best: the National Cancer Institute reports that the average American ate 7.4 lb. of carrots in 1992 (up from 6 lb. in 1980), 4 lb. of green peppers (up from 2.7 lb.), 3 lb. of broccoli (up form 1.3 lb.), 2 lb. of cauliflower (up from 1 lb.).

The bad news is the same as it has always been: the choice of vegetables in restaurants is minimal (when was the last time you saw parsnip or turnip offered?—yet we devour them every Easter, Thanksgiving and Christmas at least), and outside the expensive places, the way of preparation remains brutally unimaginative. Limp, beaten, flooded mush is the common end product, by which time virtually all the nutrients will have been flogged out of it. The result of such systematic torture visited on a slightly higher order of nature would excite the most strenuous attentions of Amnesty International.

But we digress. No need for those attentions in the home kitchen, of course.

SAUTÉ OF WILD MUSHROOMS

Basic stuff. Varieties differ in cooking time required for tenderness, and also in the amount of juices released. Never overcook mushrooms; it toughens them.

1 1/2 lb. wild mushrooms (shiitake, oyster, chanterelle)

2 tbsp. olive oil

2 tbsp. butter

2 shallots, minced

1 tbsp. balsamic vinegar

Salt and freshly ground pepper

l tbsp. finely chopped parsley (optional)

Clean and trim mushrooms, slicing into pieces of equal size. Heat oil and butter in a large skillet over medium-high heat; add shallots and cook to soften. Toss in mushrooms; cook, stirring frequently, until softened and nicely browned and juices have evaporated. Deglaze pan with vinegar. Season with salt and pepper. Sprinkle with parsley and serve at once.
Serves 4.

Variation: Wild Mushroom Sauce
Proceed as above, but remove cooked mushrooms from pan with a slotted spoon and set aside. Add 2 tbsp. brandy to pan, scraping up cooking juices. Ignite, shaking pan carefully while flame subsides. Increase heat to high, add 1 1/2 cups dry red wine (or half wine, half stock), and reduce to about half. Off heat, swirl in a few tablespoons butter to make a smooth sauce. Combine with reserved mushrooms; adjust seasoning. Quite robust, so best with game, chicken or lamb.

EGGPLANT BHARTA

Indian spices added to vegetables gives them a new dimension.

3 lb. eggplants (about 2 medium)

3 tbsp. vegetable oil or clarified butter

2 onions, finely chopped

2 cloves garlic, finely chopped

1-inch piece fresh ginger, peeled and finely chopped

1 small green chili, finely chopped

1 tbsp. ground coriander

1 tsp. ground turmeric

1 tsp. cumin seeds, crushed

1 tsp. garam masala (optional)

Juice of 1/2 lemon

1 tbsp. finely chopped coriander for garnish

Salt

Prick eggplants in several places and place on baking sheet. Bake at 350°F for 45 minutes, or until well softened. Halve, scoop out all pulp and coarsely chop; discard skins. Heat oil in a large skillet over medium heat. Add onions, garlic and ginger; fry until golden brown. Add chili, ground coriander, turmeric and cumin; cook 2 minutes. Reduce heat to low. Stir in chopped eggplant; cook gently 10 minutes (add a little water or oil if mixture gets too dry). Stir in garam masala and lemon juice. Garnish with coriander.
Serves 6.

Tip: Chop finely in a food processor and serve chilled with Parmesan Toast (*p. 26*) as an appetizer.

ALL MANNER OF VEGETABLE CHILI

Our favorite bar food, based on a chili served at the Soho Kitchen in New York City. Though perhaps it's the choice of the 100 beers or so to go with it.

Southwest Chilies:
*These dried chilies
are readily avail-
able. Make paste as
explained on p. 60,
combine and
experiment, or use
on their own.*
Ancho: *dried
poblano chili, long,
wide, dark reddish
brown, smooth
and flat.*
Chipotle: *dried
smoked jalapeño,
short, round,
crinkled, lightish
brown.*
New Mexican: *long,
smooth, dark red—
very popular in
New Mexico and
California—the
variety that is
made into brilliant
garlands.*

4 tbsp. vegetable oil

1 onion, coarsely chopped

2 cloves garlic, chopped

2 tbsp. corn flour (optional)

2 tbsp. New Mexican chili paste (*recipe follows*)

1 tbsp. chili powder

1 tsp. ground cumin

1 tsp. oregano

1 can (28 oz.) plum tomatoes

2 bay leaves

2 to 4 cups assorted cooked beans and peas
    (black, adzuki, romano)

1 sweet yellow pepper, roasted, peeled and chopped

1 sweet red pepper, roasted, peeled and chopped

2 medium zucchini, cubed

2 cups coarsely chopped cauliflower

2 cups cubed carrots

1 stalk celery, sliced

1 cup corn kernels (fresh is best)

1 tbsp. chopped coriander

Gently cook onion and garlic in oil to soften. Stir in corn flour, chili paste and chili powder, cumin and oregano; cook briefly to release flavors. Stir in tomatoes, bay leaves and beans. Simmer, uncovered, 20 minutes. Add veggies; cook and brew until very tender, 1 to 1 1/2 hours. Discard bay leaves. Stir in coriander. Serve with all manner of goodies: sour cream, chopped avocado, diced tomato and onion, shredded Cheddar and/or Monterey Jack cheese.
Serves 6 to 8.

Variation: Add 2 chorizo or Chinese sausages, sliced, halfway through cooking.

Tip: If using canned beans, drain and rinse. Add just 20 minutes before chili is cooked. Chili may be frozen.

New Mexican Chili Paste:
Soften chilies in warm water. Drain, reserving water. Remove seeds and stem. Purée with 1 to 2 tbsp. reserved water to form a paste. Press through a sieve. Better still, turn them briefly over direct heat to soften before soaking, being careful not to burn them. This may also be done in the oven. Warm chilies at 325°F for 2 to 3 minutes.

*H*OME FRIES

No food or title has been more debased in public kitchens. The best home fries, comfort food par excellence, are personal. These are ours.

1 well-seasoned cast-iron skillet

1 open wood fire

1 small island

4 medium cooking potatoes

4 tbsp. clarified butter (1/2 regular butter and half oil
   will do nicely)

2 green onions, finely chopped or 2 tbsp. snipped chives

1/4 cup chopped onions

1 tbsp. paprika

Salt and freshly ground pepper

The absolute best way to cook home fries is in the open air, with a cast-iron skillet. If the wood fire and island are not available at the moment, and the open air looks as if you could cut it in chunks, at least use the proper pan. Cook potatoes gently in simmering water until just tender; drain, cool, peel, slice. Heat butter in skillet, into which place potatoes lovingly—don't just drop them in. Sprinkle with green onions, chopped onion and paprika. Cook on one side until just browned, then turn gently and continue browning. Dust with salt and pepper. Serve them forth.

Enough for one, if nobody catches you at it.

POTATO AND ONION GALETTE

Rich, crisp and decadent.

5 to 6 tbsp. clarified butter

2 lb. (6 medium) waxy potatoes, peeled and sliced paper-thin

1 small onion, sliced paper-thin

Salt and freshly ground pepper

1 tsp. grated lemon rind

2 cloves garlic, minced

1 tbsp. finely chopped fresh rosemary

Brush 9-inch glass pie plate with 2 tbsp. clarified butter. Dry potato slices well and arrange a layer in overlapping circles to cover bottom. Top with a thin layer of onions. Drizzle with 1 tbsp. clarified butter, salt, pepper and some of the lemon rind, garlic and rosemary. Repeat to make three layers. Bake at 400°F, covered, for 10 minutes. Uncover, and press down once or twice until bottom is crisp and golden and potatoes are cooked through, about 30 minutes. Halfway through cooking, drain off excess butter, if necessary.

Serves 4.

Clarified Butter: To clarify, melt 1/2 lb. butter very slowly. Skim off froth on top. Gently pour off clear liquid, leaving milk residue on bottom. This butter will withstand higher temperatures in cooking (1/4 cup butter=7 tbsp., approximately).

SWEET POTATO CRISPS

Deep-frying root vegetables has become the latest trendy food sport, from sweet potatoes to beets to yucca. It's simple, and great for presentation. Sweet potatoes are particularly good done this way. They stay very crisp if cut in thin shoestring strips or shaved with a vegetable peeler, as below.

2 sweet potatoes, peeled

Oil for deep-frying

Salt to taste

Using a vegetable peeler, shave long strips from sweet potato, turning as you go. Deep-fry strips in hot oil 1 to 2 minutes or longer, until very crisp. Drain on paper towel. Salt. These may be prepared ahead 1 hour and reheated on a baking sheet at 350°F for 5 minutes.

Long beans and chinese sausage

Although long beans are gnarled and wrinkled, they remain crisp and flavorful when cooked. Available at Chinese markets.

l lb. Chinese long beans (or fresh green beans)

2 tbsp. peanut oil

2 cloves garlic

l tsp. crushed Szechuan peppercorns

2 whole dried red hot chilies

2 Chinese sausages, in 1/4-inch slices

l tbsp. oyster sauce

l tsp. soy sauce

l tbsp. rice wine vinegar

l tsp. sesame oil

1/4 cup chicken stock (not salty)

Szechuan Peppercorns:
Toast lightly in a dry frying pan. Rub through a sieve after crushing.

Trim beans. Blanch, dry well and slice in 2-inch pieces. Heat oil in a wok or large skillet over medium-high heat. Add beans, garlic, peppercorns, chilies and sausage. Toss and cook briskly 1 to 2 minutes. Combine remaining ingredients. Add to pan. Cook vigorously until nicely sauced but most stock has evaporated.
Serves 4.

APINI

The sweetness of tomato contrasts well with the slight bitterness of the rapini and the pungent taste of the basil.

2 tbsp. fruity olive oil

1 clove garlic, minced

1 onion, finely chopped

2 tomatoes, peeled, seeded and chopped, or equivalent canned

1 tbsp. chopped basil

1/2 lb. rapini, rinsed, rough stems removed, coarsely chopped

Salt and freshly ground pepper to taste

Squirt of lemon juice

Heat oil in a large, heavy skillet. Toss in garlic and onion and sauté until softened. Add tomatoes and basil; cook 2 to 3 minutes. Add rapini and toss well. Cover and cook until rapini is tender, about 5 minutes. Remove cover and let juices cook off. Season with salt, pepper and lemon juice.
Serves 4 to 6.

Antipasto

An admirable combination livening all the senses; each vegetable retains its own character. Serve with crisp homemade toasts.

1 cup chopped onions

2 cups chopped carrots

1/4 lb. broad green beans, cut in 1-inch lengths

1/2 cauliflower, cut in small pieces

1 sweet green pepper, seeded and chopped

Salt

1 cup white wine vinegar

1 cup vegetable oil

1/2 cup olive oil

1 can (7 oz.) solid white tuna in water, drained

12 artichoke hearts (halved and cooked), or canned

1/2 lb. mushrooms, sliced

1/4 lb. Italian green olives, pitted

5 tbsp. tomato paste

1 tbsp. paprika

Persons living entirely on vegetables are seldom of a plump and succulent habit. —William Cullen, 1774.

Place each vegetable in a separate bowl and toss lightly with salt. Let stand covered overnight at room temperature. In a large pot, whisk together vinegar, vegetable oil and olive oil. Bring to a boil over moderate heat. Add onions; cook for 5 minutes. Continue adding remaining vegetables one at a time; cook until just tender. Remove from heat. Break tuna into small chunks in a bowl. Toss with cooked vegetables, artichoke hearts, mushrooms, olives, tomato paste and paprika. Chill for 3 hours. Serve on a bed of lettuce or as a snack with crispy toasts. Keep refrigerated one week.

Makes 6 cups.

PANZANELLA

A savory salad and a rustic staple in southern Italy.

1 clove garlic, minced

1 tbsp. minced capers

2 anchovies, minced

Croûtons (*recipe follows*)

1/4 cup extra virgin olive oil

1 tbsp. red wine vinegar

1/2 cup finely chopped sweet red pepper

6 plum tomatoes, chopped

1/2 English cucumber, seeded and diced

1 cup diced red onion

1/2 cup diced celery

1/4 cup finely chopped parsley

1 tbsp. finely chopped fresh basil

Lemon juice, pepper and salt

Mash garlic, capers, anchovies and three croûtons to a paste; whisk in oil and vinegar. Toss with pepper, tomatoes, cucumber, onion, celery, herbs and remaining croûtons. Season to taste and drizzle over extra oil if desired. Let stand 1 hour to allow flavors to meld.
Serves 6 to 8.

Croûtons
6 cups firm Italian bread, cut in 1/2-inch cubes.
Arrange bread cubes on a baking sheet. Lightly toast at 300°F for 20 minutes until golden brown and crisp. Let cool.

Tip: Celery is much better if peeled first, like carrots, with a vegetable peeler.

Minted Lentil Salad

1 1/2 cups lentils (preferably le puy), rinsed

1 medium carrot, peeled and diced

1 clove garlic, finely chopped

1 bay leaf

1 celery top

1/2 tsp. salt

1 sweet red pepper, roasted, peeled and chopped

1 sweet yellow pepper, roasted, peeled and chopped

1/4 cup chopped green onion

1/4 cup chopped parsley

1 tbsp. chopped fresh mint

Lemon Vinaigrette (*recipe follows*)

Salt and freshly ground pepper to taste

Thin lemon slices and additional herbs for garnish

In a medium saucepan, cover lentils with water by 2 inches; add carrot, garlic, bay leaf, celery and salt. Bring to boil, lower heat and simmer about 20 minutes, until lentils are tender but still retain their shape. Drain, discarding bay leaf and celery. Toss with peppers, onion, parsley, mint and vinaigrette. Cover and let stand 1 hour. Stir in pepper and salt. Serve garnished with lemon slices, additional herbs, perhaps on greens or topped with crumbled feta.
Serves 6.

Lemon Vinaigrette

1 clove garlic, minced

1/4 tsp. salt

2 tbsp. lemon juice

1/4 tsp. cumin

Pinch cayenne

6 tbsp. extra virgin olive oil

Combine garlic, salt, lemon juice, cumin and cayenne. Whisk in oil.

BLACK-EYED PEA SALAD

Greece is uncommonly rich in legume and vegetable dishes, due—
still—to frequent church-declared meatless days.

1 1/2 cups dried black-eyed peas

1/2 small red onion, finely chopped

1/2 cup finely chopped Italian parsley

1 clove garlic, minced

1 tbsp. red wine vinegar

2 tbsp extra virgin olive oil

Salt and freshly ground pepper to taste

3 large ripe tomatoes, peeled, seeded, roughly chopped

1 tsp. balsamic vinegar

2 tbsp. fresh basil

*Soak peas in cold water to cover overnight; drain. In a saucepan,
cover with fresh water, bring to a boil and cook 10 minutes; drain.
Cover again with fresh water, bring to a boil, lower heat and simmer
about 30 minutes, until tender; drain. Toss with onion, parsley, garlic,
red wine vinegar, 1 tbsp. oil, salt and pepper. Set aside. Shortly before
serving, toss tomatoes with remaining oil, balsamic vinegar, basil, salt
and pepper; gently fold in beans.*
Serves 6.

CORN

ORARE BEN FRANKLIN! THAT HUMANE AND COMMON-sensical man, famous kite flier and inventor of bifocals, was also right, ineluctably and incontrovertibly right, about corn. He liked it, and being who he was, let anyone who questioned the fact know just where his heart stood on the matter.

Late in 1765 a spate of letters ran in the London, England, *Gazetteer* concerning taxes in the colonies, particularly the troublesome tax on tea. One writer suggested that if Americans disliked the tax so much, all they had to do was drink no more tea. Impossible, replied a respondent: what else would Americans start the day with? Their Indian corn, he opined, "does not afford an agreeable or easily digestible breakfast."

Cue Ben Franklin, living in London at the time. Reading this slur, doubtless through his bifocals, he at once put pen to paper.

"Pray let me, an American," he wrote in the *Gazetteer* on January 2, 1766, "inform the gentleman, who seems ignorant of the matter, that Indian corn, take it for all in all, is one of the most agreeable and wholesome grains in the world"—and added, ominously, that the respondent's letter, and the ones before it, would serve only "to strengthen us in every resolution of advantage—to *our* country, at least, if not *yours*."

Ten years later Franklin was one of the signatories who wrote the cultivation and enjoyment of corn into the Declaration of Independence (under a little-known codicil to the Pursuit of Happiness, annotated in Ben's spidery hand: "Add, Self-Evident Truths").

It may be thought the victory was one-sided, since large parts of Europe—notably France, Germany and Britain—still disdain the stuff except as maize, which they use as pig and cattle fodder; globally, less than a quarter of the world's corn supply goes to humans.

Would that more victories were so one-sided! Let the heathen bask in ignorance. If their grasp of the pleasure principle is so tenuous, they deserve no better. The rest of us can go on relishing what the Indians knew long before Ben Franklin: that corn in all its glory is one of the great boons and blessings of the human race.

And it is the Indians, once again, we have most to thank. Five thousand years before Christ, they were cultivating the wild grass that evolved into *Zea mays* (maize), and thence to *Zea saccharata*, the sweet corn that has adorned our summers for a century and a half. A cultigen, *Zea* must be seeded every year, and its wild progenitor has been long extinct. A wisp of it, a botanical smudge, was found in the form of 19 grains of fossilized wild-corn pollens, 200 feet under Mexico City as the foundation was being dug for a skyscraper. That was in 1954. The pollen itself scientists found harder to date: 25,000 to 80,000 years old, they hazarded generously.

So to today. Forget the eons if one must. This splendid plant, rich in protein, potassium and phosphorus, is a buttress of more immediate North American heritages. Corn feeds us all—if not, through some aberrant personal aversion, at first hand, then at second, through pigs, cattle, free-range chickens. The simple act of shucking corn spells and smells of summer; Americans grow up with the story of Abe Lincoln uttering his newborn squeals on a corn-shuck mattress.

Later, dekerneled, the cobs have been used for everything from fire kindling to home insulation, from jug stoppers to back scratchers, tool handles to scrubbing brushes. Corn oil illuminated farmers' houses for more than a century and fueled lighthouse lanterns on the Great Lakes 130 years ago; purified, it is a zero-cholesterol, polyunsaturated kitchen standard today; alcoholized and combined with gasoline, it economically forms gasohol, a staple at cut-rate gas pumps in the United States and much of Latin America.

And breathes there a man with soul so bred that he has never found himself in an outhouse happily using nature's own tubular toilet roll piled on the handy shelf? Something else we learned from the Indians.

Provided you can get it really fresh—the only way to enjoy it at its fullest—corn straight off the cob is the *ne plus ultra*, both ears and the tail; shamelessly messy, butter dripping off the chin, chilled beer within reach, God's earth beneath, His open sky above. End-of-summer festivals abound in small towns of the corn country: one we stumbled across in southern Ontario, a quintessential country fair complete with Little League playoffs and Japanese lanterns strung in trees, keeps a massive cauldron at the simmer during corn-harvest, and every hour or so dispatches a truck to the cornfields to return laden with cobs of exemplary freshness.

Freshness in most things we eat is, at the least, desirable; with corn it is the be-all and end-all. The graph goes like this: corn fresh from the field tastes like CORN; six-hour-old corn tastes like CORN; day-old corn tastes like corn; three-day-old corn tastes like nothing at all. This is because the sugar in sweet corn turns rapidly, once picked, to starch. The commercial result is that much corn sold on city vegetable counters at harvest time is only worth it if you buy early in the day and cook at once; and that none of the plastic-wrapped ears sold in and out of season at supermarkets will ever be worth a fiddler's farthing.

Cooking it: Everyone can sling cobs into a boiling pot for a few minutes and then get at it, aided only by a dish of cold butter to roll them in, and a salt shaker. But for cooking *with* corn:

Corn kernels—Place husked corn stem down. Cut from top to bottom, not too close to the core, 3 or 4 rows at a time.

Creamed corn—Cook 2 cups of fresh kernels in a little butter. Add 1 cup cream. Heat through. Whirl in a blender or food processor until just creamed.

YOUR VERY BASIC CORN

For those who haven't been paying attention, or who have always had their teeth brushed for them in the past and now want to do their own for a change.

1 pair running shoes

1 convenient farm

1 large cauldron

Water and milk (half and half)

Corn, as much as it takes

Sugar, sprinkle of

Butter, plenty of

Napkins, blizzard of

Salt and pepper

I'd rather talk about corn than anything else.
—Paul Christoph Mangelsdorf (1899-1989), Harvard botany professor and (for more than 60 years) devout corn breeder.

Don running shoes. Ensure all hindrances between you and the corn-field are minor or, better still, nonexistent. Bring cauldron of water/milk to boil, yourself to a simmer. Now! think how Carl Lewis would have done it and emulate him as closely as nature allows. Dash to field, everything pumping furiously, grab corn, dash back to cauldron. Husk madly. Drop the corn into the pot and switch off the heat the instant the liquid returns to the boil. Allow the ears to sit no less than 5 minutes, no more than 20: small, if maddening, price to pay for nirvana. And then, accept the homage of your friends, for you deserve it.

SAUSAGE CORNBREAD

Sausage baked in cornbread batter: a great treat. Serve with assorted mustards, pickles and chutneys.

1 cup yellow cornmeal

1 cup all-purpose flour

2 tbsp. sugar

1 tsp. salt

1/2 tsp. baking soda

2 tsp. baking powder

1 tsp. dried basil

1 egg, beaten

1 1/2 cups buttermilk

1/4 cup shredded Cheddar cheese

1/4 cup melted butter

1 lb. cooked, cooled spicy sausage (kielbasa, pepperoni, hot Italian; enough to fit the length of an 8-inch loaf pan), peeled if casing is heavy.

In a large bowl, combine cornmeal, flour, sugar, salt, baking soda, baking powder and basil. Blend egg with buttermilk. Stir into dry ingredients, blending quickly. Stir in Cheddar cheese and melted butter. Pour half the batter into greased loaf pan. Place sausage on top. Cover with remaining batter. Bake at 400°F for 35 to 40 minutes until loaf has risen and is set. Let rest 10 minutes before removing from pan. Slice and serve warm or cool.

SPINACH

SIXTY-FOUR YEARS AFTER IT WAS PUBLISHED IN *THE NEW Yorker*, Carl Rose's cartoon remains the most quoted, and misquoted, comment on the subject: "I say it's spinach, and I say the hell with it." A perfect Menckenite metaphor for American mistrust of smoke and mirrors. Over the years the atrabilious speaker seems to have changed in the telling from Rose's peevish eightish girl to a peevish eightish boy; and nobody remembers it was originally a dialogue, the mother trying the kind of diversionary tactic—"It's broccoli, dear"—that mothers before and since have deployed in the never-ending effort to ease the youthfully hated foliage past kids' front teeth. And all with as much success as Rose's. Curious, then, that it takes only a few more years for spinach to take its rightful, astringent place on the tables of the majority, many of whom discover soon enough that they prefer it, at last, to broccoli.

A late domestic, spinach was planted first in Persian gardens, traveled from there to China in the sixth century (Chinese for spinach translates today as Persian herb), and managed to make it to Europe, in cultivated form, only in the twelfth century. This was thanks to the Moors: tiring of circumcision and architecture, they added it to the list of things they introduced to Spain. Indeed, our word is a variant on *spinacha*, Spanish greens, by which it was known for centuries throughout western Europe.

There was a time when spinach was thought to be the cure-all to end all cure-alls—body-builder *sans pareil*, stiff with iron, potassium, calcium, vitamins and heaven knows what else. Anything so verdant, so richly pungent, had to be good for you, and make small persons fit and strong and tall; it was the idea underlying Rose's cartoon.

Well, it still is good for you but not as good as it once was. Science has been rewriting some of the claims ("I say they're spinach," said Science, and brooked no questions as usual).

When buying spinach, assess its liveliness. It should have a bouncing, bright appearance. As you stuff it into your basket or string bag, it should crunch and squeak.
—Jane Grigson, 1978.

True, spinach contains plenty of potassium, vitamin A, calcium and folic acid; it is a good source of fiber; it does contribute, in otherwise healthy bodies, to development and growth; it prevents anemia and such vitamin-deficiency diseases as scurvy. But it is also true, says Science now, that spinach's iron content—the iron that always saved Popeye and Olive Oyl in the last reel—is not as large as the propaganda, and comes in a form not easily assimilated by the body. And spinach, like rhubarb, contains oxalic acid (particularly in its uncooked spinach-salad state) and is therefore not good at all for people with kidney stones or liver and bladder ailments.

A pity about these last bits. But we should remember that to the healthy it is still a marvelous food, utterly and lastingly distinctive—"a standard," wrote the late English foodie Jane Grigson, a standard herself, "of vegetable aspiration."

Cooking with it: Raw and adorned, cooked and unadorned, are the typical preparations, but there is a wealth of other spinach experience. The leaves absorb about half their weight in butter, over time, and may be turned—damn the cholesterol—into a sublime foil for grilled or roasted meats; anything with a taste firm enough to match it.

• In addition to butter, spinach can be enhanced by eggs, cheese (ricotta, Parmesan, feta), yogurt, anchovies, mushrooms, pine nuts, nutmeg, pepper, a touch of lemon, a pinch of sugar.

• Consider spinach as a moist wrapping for small fish.

• 1 lb. fresh spinach yields about 1 cup cooked; just enough for two as a vegetable.

• Never cook spinach in an iron or aluminum pot: it quickly picks up a nasty metallic taste. Serve in glass or porcelain (and not silver) for the same reason. Always keep cooking time to a minimum.

• Basic preparation: Trim, wash carefully free of grit. Remove tougher stalks. Cook 3 to 5 minutes in a steamer over a small amount of water; or 5 minutes in a large covered pan over moderate heat and in no water at all. Stir from time to time so that the bottom layer does not burn, and remember Popeye the mighty-muscled Sailorman, who yis what he yis thanks above all to *Spinacia oleracea.*

SPINACH RAITA

A delicious Indian side dish for curried or grilled meats.

1 tsp. ground roasted cumin seed

1 tsp. ground roasted coriander seed

1/4 tsp. freshly ground pepper

Pinch cayenne

1/2 cup plain yogurt

10 oz. spinach, well washed, stems removed

Salt to taste

Sugar to taste

Paprika

Stir cumin, coriander, pepper and cayenne into yogurt; set aside. Place wet spinach in a large, heavy saucepan, with a little water; cover and set over moderate heat. After 2 minutes, stir so bottom layer doesn't burn. Lower heat and cook a minute or 2 more until uniformly tender. Drain and cool; squeeze to remove excess liquid. Chop spinach; stir into yogurt. Season to taste with salt and sugar; sprinkle with paprika. Serves 4.

Variation: For Cucumber Raita, use 1/2 English cucumber in place of spinach. Halve and seed cucumber, cutting in very thin slices. Dust with salt (1/2 tsp.). Leave for 10 minutes and then gently squeeze out excess juice.

SPINACH WITH CURRIED LENTILS

A dish undreamed of in Popeye's philosophy. Excellent with a cool cucumber raita.

2 cups dried lentils

1 1/2 cups water

1 small onion, chopped

3 cloves garlic, finely chopped

3 slices fresh ginger, peeled

2 bay leaves

2 dry red chilies

1 tsp. turmeric

4 cups chopped fresh spinach

Salt to taste

A squeeze of lemon juice

Olive oil

Rinse lentils. Add to pot with water and bring to boil. Stir in onion, garlic, ginger, bay leaves, dry chilies and turmeric. Cover and cook 15 minutes. Stir in spinach and continue cooking another 15 minutes until lentils are tender. Season to taste with salt, lemon juice and a drop or two of olive oil.
Serves 8.

LETTUCE

WE HAVE TAKEN LETTUCE TOO LONG FOR GRANTED. Month in, year out, lettuce has always been there, even when it was almost always iceberg and 96 percent water. But that was ages ago (the seventies, anyway), and now the supermarkets groan with choice. Bibb, Boston, romaine, arugula, endive, escarole, radicchio and then some; all this without mentioning bland old iceberg—still among the 10 most popular vegetables in North America—more than twice. Something has been going on here that the emperor Diocletian would have appreciated.

An exceptional military administrator, Diocletian was not big on Christians (he persecuted them) or imperial agricultural policy (it was disastrous). But he was the only emperor to step down of his own accord when he'd had enough (in the year 305), the better to devote his remaining years to see if he could manage his own vegetable patch better than the empire's.

History suggests that indeed he could, and that when Maximian, a successor, pleaded with him to return and share the empire-ruling chores with him, Diocletian genially replied: "If you saw the beautiful lettuces I'm raising, you wouldn't ask such an idiot question." If only politicians today had so nice a sense of proportion!

Not that Diocletian was a lettuce pioneer. The ancient Egyptians seem to have started it, since lettuce was sacred to the great Min, Egyptian god of increase, perhaps because the milky lettuce juice, which it shares with its close relative the dandelion, was symbolically maternal. (Less is heard of Max, Egyptian god of decrease. One can only wonder why.) The Egyptians were also probably the first to cultivate romaine (cos, as it is sometimes called) on the island of Kos, off the coast of what is now Turkey. They knew—as Hippocrates the oath-giver and father of medicine, and himself a native of

Kos, also knew—that all lettuce is good for the eyes, skin, bones and blood.

Except, surely, iceberg, which is put to its best use by Chinese restaurants in rainbow-chopped-in-crystal-fold, and to its worst by restaurants like McDonald's and Mr. Submarine, shredding it into tiny pieces that somehow manage to work their way into curious parts of your clothing.

Salad greens of the lettuce family, and relatives by marriage, may be white, pale green, dark green or purple, and they fall roughly into two flavor groups.

MILD:
- *Bibb*—Small head lettuce; dark green, soft, loose leaves; sweet, delicate.
- *Boston*—Larger head lettuce, similar leaves; sweet, succulent.
- *Iceberg*—Enough already, except that it has come to be prized in parts of Europe that may have grown tired of everything else.
- *Lamb's lettuce* (mâche)—Spoon-shaped leaves, melting texture; slightly astringent.
- *Leaf*—Longish leaves that grow loose without forming a head; crisper than Boston; particularly fresh-tasting.
- *Red leaf*—A favorite of chefs and gardeners: curly, attractive.
- *Romaine* (cos)—Upright, stiff leaves; crisp texture; tart.

BITTER:
- *Arugula*—Known as rocket to our ancestors, who let it lapse because of its brief shelf life, it has been reintroduced to us from the Mediterranean. Smooth, dark green; sharply peppery, with a hint of walnut when young; overbitter when mature.
- *Belgian endive* (witloof chicory)—An accident in a Belgian greenhouse when a gardener discovered, in the 1840s, that chicory roots covered in soil became firm, white, tightly furled shoots with a delectable crispness and a sharply pungent flavor.
- *Curly endive*—Loose leaves, pale yellow and small at the center, dark green on the outside, crinkly edges; crisp, tart.
- *Dandelion*—Much better known as food and wine to our grandparents, it deserves better than the mindless hate generally leveled at it today by those gardeners who save their love for lawns. Small young leaves give a marvelously astringent bite to a green salad.
- *Escarole*—Flat-leaved close kin to the curly endive. Dark green, fleshy leaves turning to crisply pale at the center; firm, sharp.
- *Radicchio*—Firm, redheaded relative of Belgian endive, but less crisp. Some radicchio (verona) looks like small cabbage, white stem and ribs, reddish leaves. Others are slender and tapered. All lend a distinctive crisp tang to a salad; bitterness increases with age.
- *Watercress*—An aquatic plant with small, delicate, dark green leaves; sharp, pungent, peppery; particularly good in sandwiches with almost anything.

FIELD SALAD
WITH WARM SHIITAKE MUSHROOMS

The greens available today make it possible to produce the most remarkable salads. This is our favorite combination—a Renaissance salad of many dimensions.

In the composure of a salad, every plant should come in to bear its part, without being overpowered by some herb of a stronger taste... but fall into their places, like the notes in music, in which there should be nothing harsh or grating... though admitting some discords, to distinguish and illustrate the rest. —John Evelyn, English diarist-gourmet, as right today as he was in 1699.

The greens:

2 handfuls mixed baby greens

2 oz. mâche (2 handfuls)

2 oz. frisée (1 handful)

1 head Boston lettuce

1 bunch arugula

Wash greens; dry well. Tear if necessary. Wrap in towel and refrigerate until ready to use. Any combination of greens will do. This one is particularly good.

The dressing:

3 tbsp. olive oil

1 tbsp. balsamic vinegar

1 shallot, finely chopped

2 cloves garlic, sliced in three

1/4 tsp. salt

1/4 tsp. freshly ground pepper

Combine ingredients. Whisk well. Let stand 1 hour or more. Remove garlic before using.

The mushrooms:

3/4 lb. fresh shiitake mushrooms

1 shallot, finely chopped

2 tbsp. fruity olive oil

1 tbsp. balsamic vinegar

Salt to taste

Discard stems from mushrooms. Slice mushrooms thinly. In a skillet over moderate heat, sauté mushrooms and shallots in olive oil to soften. Add balsamic vinegar (will instantly reduce); season with salt. (Mushrooms may be cooked ahead of time. Reheat and deglaze with vinegar just before serving.)

To serve: whisk dressing well, strain. Toss a tablespoon at a time with greens (use your hands to mix). Divide among six plates. Top with warm mushrooms. Serve with freshly ground pepper.

Serves 6.

DANDELION SALAD

1 lb. dandelion leaves, well washed

1 fennel bulb

2 tbsp. lemon juice

4 tbsp. olive oil

Yolk of a hard-cooked egg, sieved

1/4 lb. mushrooms, thinly sliced

1/4 tsp. Dijon mustard

Salt and pepper to taste

To make a good salad is to be a brilliant diplomatist—the problem is entirely the same in both cases. To know how much oil one must mix with one's vinegar.
—Oscar Wilde, 1880.

Tear the dandelion leaves into bite-sized pieces. Remove core and outside stalk from fennel bulb and slice thinly. Blend lemon juice, oil and egg until quite smooth. Beat in mustard, salt and pepper. Toss everything together.

Serves 4 to 6.

Note: Pick your own dandelion leaves in early spring before they have flowered. There is nothing quite like the tender new shoots—just be sure you know where your neighbors' dogs take their daily stroll.

Pasta and Grains

PASTA

WE ASSOCIATE PASTA INDELIBLY WITH ITALY: AFTER all, it is an Italian word and Italians from Boccaccio to Caruso, Dante to Tetrazzini, Garibaldi to Pope John XXIII, Antonio Bomba and six centuries of countrymen besides, have endowed it with a national mysticism the rest of us wouldn't generally go looking for in ground wheat kernels.

Italians make such an extravagant fuss about it, in song and story, that Detective Plodd of the Fraud Squad (semolina detail) might wonder if collectively they have something to hide. In historical fact, nobody knows for sure, despite the most serious searches, where pasta originated. Some say China (always a logical option), the Venetian Marco Polo bringing a crate of it back from his Asian adventures in the thirteenth century. Japan also lays claim to it, followed by Germany and France. Koreans say a pox on all Japanese houses, since they taught them the art of making *soba* noodles—a traditional gift of welcome in Japan for the past 400 years—some time in the twelfth century.

Italians counter that the Roman poet Horace (just before Christ) and the wit Martial (just after Him) both wrote persuasively about "little pastas"; others retort that this is a misreading (by Italian translators, naturally) of the Roman word *pastilla*, translated by everyone else as *small round cakes*.

Still, we can say that Naples was the first place to produce pasta on an industrial scale. That was early in the fifteenth century, and the industry was local since the pasta was fresh and did not travel. The technique for drying it (*pasta asciutta*) was not developed for another 400 years; today, good-quality dried pasta is every bit as good, to our taste, as modern fresh (and newly fashionable) pasta, and in fact its flavor and texture enable it to blend with sauces rather better.

Spaghetti, macaroni, fettuccine, tagliatelle, sheets of lasagna, stuffed ravioli: main-course staples thanks to Naples, as much a part of our kitchens as bacon and eggs. Of the countless other variants, the small shapes—such as anellini (little rings), pennette (small quills), conchigliette (tiny shells)—work well in clear soups or light salads, tossed with fresh herbs and fresh or canned seafood; and the heavy, ribbed pastas like penne, rotini, rigatoni and fusilli hold sauces well and are robust enough to withstand baking and reheating.

But for the basic pastas, boiling is the order of the day. And what can go wrong with that? Two things only: too small a pot, and boiling too long. Each 4 oz. of pasta needs a hit of salt and at least 1 qt. of water to boil it in: any less, and the water won't be able to circulate freely around the pasta, which will then cook unevenly and stick together. A tablespoon of olive oil in the water will add flavor. Cook at a steady boil, stirring betimes; after three or four minutes, start testing. When still a bit firm (*al dente*), remove from heat (it will continue cooking a little), drain quickly, toss with sauce and serve at once. *Forza Italia!*

Classic Tomato Sauce

This essentially Italian variation was taught to us by Linda Caputo, in Sault Ste. Marie, Ontario, who learned it from her mother, who. . . . Serve over freshly cooked pasta, or spoon over firm white fish or grilled chicken breasts.

1/4 cup fruity olive oil

1 small onion, finely chopped (1/2 cup)

2 cloves garlic, minced

1/4 cup minced carrot

1/4 cup minced celery

2 cans (each 28 oz.) plum tomatoes, well drained and chopped

Sprigs of fresh thyme and rosemary

1 bay leaf

1 tbsp. finely chopped fresh basil

1 tbsp. finely chopped parsley

Squeeze lemon juice

Salt and freshly ground pepper to taste

Before serving, add cold water to pot of boiling pasta— when al dente. This prevents over-cooking and lends a few moments breathing time.

Heat oil in a heavy skillet. Toss in onion, garlic, carrot and celery. Simmer briskly to soften. (Vegetables are not sautéed but rather boiled in the oil.) Do not let brown. Add tomatoes, thyme, rosemary and bay leaf. Let mixture stew contentedly over low heat until reduced and lightly thickened, about 20 minutes. Stir in basil and parsley. Season with lemon juice, salt and pepper. Discard bay leaf.
Makes 2 1/2 cups.

Variation: 1) Add 1/2 cup vermouth when sauce is thickened. Reduce briefly. 2) Swirl in 1/2 cup 35% cream. Let reduce to nicely thicken. 3) Stir in 1/2 tsp. saffron threads soaked in wine or a little water towards end of cooking. 4) A combination of any or all the above. 5) Add 1 tbsp. finely minced banana pepper when cooking onion mixture.

SICILIAN FISH SAUCE

Thick, pungent, fragrant, this is a marvellous winter sauce for pasta.

4 tbsp. olive oil

1 large onion, chopped

4 cloves garlic, minced

1 fennel bulb, chopped

1 tsp. dried basil (or a sprig of fresh)

1 can (14 oz.) tomatoes, puréed

1/2 tsp. salt and freshly ground pepper

1 tbsp. sugar

1 cup raisins

2 cans (each 3 1/4 oz.) skinless, boneless sardines

1/2 cup pine nuts

1 lb. fettucine or spaghetti

Seasoned breadcrumbs (optional)

Heat oil in a large saucepan. Cook onion, garlic, fennel and basil until softened. Purée in a food processor and return to pot. Add tomatoes, salt, pepper, sugar, raisins and 1 can sardines. Simmer gently 40 minutes. Remove from heat and stir in second can of sardines and pine nuts. Refrigerate overnight. Reheat over medium heat. Cook pasta in a large pot of boiling salted water until al dente. Drain well. Spoon sauce over pasta; toss well and, if desired, sprinkle the whole lot with breadcrumbs seasoned with olive oil, garlic, parsley, salt and pepper. Serves 6.

Hearty Seafood and Rotini

This dish is a labor of love. Resist the temptation to simmer the vegetables and seafood all together: the result will be too thin to adhere well to pasta.

2 1/2 cups Classic Tomato Sauce with saffron and vermouth
    (*recipe on p. 85*)

1/2 small red onion, halved and thinly sliced

1/2 sweet red pepper, halved and thinly sliced

1/2 sweet yellow pepper, halved and thinly sliced

1/2 lb. mushrooms (preferably a mixture of shiitake, oyster
    and button)

1/2 cup pitted black olives

Salt and freshly ground pepper to taste

Squeeze lemon juice

2 tbsp. butter

1/2 lb. shrimp, peeled

3/4 lb. bay scallops, patted dry

A dozen or more mussels, scrubbed clean and soaked

1 lb. rotini, cooked

Freshly grated Parmesan cheese

In skillet over medium heat, sauté onions, peppers and mushrooms in oil until just softened. Stir in olives. Season with salt, pepper and lemon juice. Set aside. Melt butter in a large sauté pan or skillet over high heat. (Relax and have a sip or two of wine.) Toss in shrimp; cook briefly until nicely plump and pink, slightly underdone. Transfer shrimp to a bowl. Toss in scallops, flipping once or twice until they're done. Add to shrimp. Pour a splash or two of whatever you are drinking (ideally white wine) into the pan. Add mussels. Clamp on lid. Shake and toss until mussels just open. Set aside. Discard any mussels that have not opened. Heat tomato sauce. Toss 1/2 cup with cooked pasta.

Needless to say, timing is a little critical here. Gently stir seafood (without juices) into remaining sauce. Simmer 1 or 2 minutes just to warm. Reheat vegetables briefly. Spoon pasta onto warm plates. Top with lots of sauce and seafood. Pile vegetables on top. Serve with freshly grated Parmesan cheese and lots of freshly ground pepper. Serves 6.

VEAL CANNELLONI

A fine dish for a crowd—easy to make in advance and, rare for pasta, it stands reheating.

12 cooked cannelloni, cooled

Veal Filling (*recipe follows*)

2 1/2 cups Classic Tomato Sauce (*recipe on p. 85*)

1 cup shredded mozzarella cheese

2 tbsp. grated Parmesan cheese

Tuck about 2 tbsp. veal filling into each cannelloni. Lightly oil a baking dish, drizzle with a little tomato sauce (1 cup), and arrange filled cannelloni in a single layer. Spoon remaining sauce on top; sprinkle with mozzarella and Parmesan cheeses. Bake at 350°F until hot and bubbly, about 30 minutes. Serve with a crisp green salad (bitter assorted greens would be nice) tossed in a light vinaigrette, with a bottle of Montepulciano d'Abruzzo.
Serves 4.

Veal Filling

1 tbsp. vegetable oil

1 lb. finely ground veal or chicken

1 tbsp. butter

2 cloves garlic, minced

1 small onion, minced

2 tbsp. minced carrot

2 tbsp. minced celery

1/2 tsp. freshly grated nutmeg

1/2 tsp. dried thyme

1 tbsp. finely chopped parsley

1 tbsp. finely chopped fresh basil

1 egg, beaten

1 tbsp. grated Parmesan cheese

1 cup creamed ricotta

Salt and freshly ground pepper to taste

In a large skillet over medium heat, cook veal in oil until just tender, breaking up meat well as you stir. Transfer with a slotted spoon to a large bowl. Drain fat from skillet; melt butter. Add garlic, onion, carrot and celery. Cook, stirring, until just softened. Toss with veal; cool slightly and then stir in remaining ingredients. Mix well.

Note: If using fresh pasta, cut pasta sheets into 4-inch squares. Drop a few at a time into a large pot of boiling salted water. Boil 1 minute. Lift out the squares, dip into cold water and drain flat on dampened towels. Place filling on one side of pasta square. Roll up and proceed as above.

WILD MUSHROOM FETTUCINE

1/2 lb. fettucine
Sauté of Wild Mushrooms (*p. 57*)
1/2 cup chicken stock
1 tbsp. chopped fresh basil
Olive oil, to taste
A squeeze of lemon juice and freshly ground pepper
2 tbsp. grated Parmesan cheese

Cook fettucine in a large pot of boiling water until just tender. Drain well. Add stock to prepared mushrooms. Toss all ingredients with pasta. Serve immediately.
Serves 4.

BARCAIOLLO'S PENNE ARRABBIATA

Lake Maggiore is a glistening deep blue lake nestled peacefully in the hills northwest of Milan. In Arona at the southern end, in a first-rate restaurant called Il Barcaiollo, one can dine on carpaccio with paper-thin slices of *parmigiano-reggiano*, crusty bread rubbed with sweet garlic and rich olive oil grilled over an open wood fire; delectable risotto with wild mushrooms and parmigiano; penne with creamy gorgonzola and various grilled seafoods including fresh salmon trout from the lake, followed with a well-chilled Pinot Grigio.

The following recipe is our version of a spicier penne pasta, excellent as an appetizer or, with the addition of grilled seafood, a main course.

1/2 lb. penne
1/4 cup extra virgin olive oil
2 cloves garlic, finely minced
4 ripe fruity tomatoes, seeded, peeled and finely chopped
  (or equivalent canned)
4 whole dried cayenne peppers

1/4 cup freshly grated Parmesan cheese
l tbsp. finely chopped Italian parsley
Lots of freshly ground pepper

Cook penne in a large pot of boiling water until al dente. Meanwhile, cook garlic in oil to soften. Add tomatoes and peppers; cook briskly until lightly thickened. Toss together well-drained pasta, hot chili sauce, Parmesan cheese and parsley. Add some more olive oil if necessary. Sprinkle with ground pepper.
Serves 4.

Tip: Olives or roasted red peppers make an excellent addition.

PESTO AND ROASTED PEPPER PASTA SALAD

Fusilli and rotini are spiral-shaped pastas that hold sauces well, as do the butterfly-shaped farfalle.

3/4 lb. fusilli
2 tbsp. fruity olive oil
1/2 cup pesto (*recipe follows*)
1 roasted red pepper, chopped
1/2 cup marinated artichoke hearts, cut in thin wedges
1/2 cup pitted black olives (preferably taggiasca)
Salt and freshly ground pepper to taste
Lemon juice to taste

Cook fusilli in a pot of boiling salted water. Drain thoroughly; toss with olive oil, then pesto. Set aside to cool. Toss with remaining ingredients.
Serves 4.

Variation: Add grilled shrimp or strips of barbecued chicken.

Pesto:

In a blender, combine 1 cup fresh basil, 2 cloves garlic, 1/3 cup toasted pine nuts or walnuts, 3/4 cup grated Parmesan cheese. Blend until smooth. Gradually beat in 1/2 cup olive oil.

SMOKED CHICKEN, BEAN AND PASTA SALAD

1/2 lb. fusilli or farfalle

Mustard Vinaigrette (*recipe follows*)

1 red onion, thinly sliced

1 sweet yellow pepper, grilled, peeled and thinly sliced

2 yellow or green zucchini, blanched and cut in chunks

1/2 lb. green beans, blanched

2 smoked, grilled or poached boned chicken breasts, sliced

Salt and freshly ground pepper to taste

Garnishes:

Cherry tomatoes, halved

Niçoise olives

Chopped fresh basil

Chopped parsley

Cook fusilli in a large pot of lightly salted boiling water until al dente; drain well. Toss in about half the vinaigrette. Cover and set aside until room temperature. Spoon pasta onto a platter; arrange vegetables and chicken on top and garnish with tomatoes, olives and herbs. Drizzle over remaining vinaigrette.
Serves 8.

Mustard Vinaigrette

3 tbsp. red wine vinegar

1 tbsp. grainy Dijon mustard

Salt and freshly ground pepper to taste

1/2 cup olive oil

Blend vinegar, mustard, salt and pepper. Slowly whisk in oil.

SPICY THAI NOODLES

One of the great Thai signature dishes, a bracing high-wire act of taste and texture.

1/2 lb. dry rice noodles

2 tbsp. fish sauce

2 tbsp. sugar

2 tbsp. cider vinegar

2 tbsp. soy sauce

1 tbsp. oyster sauce

2 tbsp. tomato ketchup

2 tbsp. oil

1 small onion, chopped

2 slices fresh ginger

2 cloves garlic, chopped

1/2 lb. boneless, skinless chicken cut in strips

1/2 lb. small shrimp, peeled and chopped

1 tbsp. pure red chili paste

2 eggs, lightly beaten

Garnishes:

1 lb. fresh bean sprouts

Lime wedges

2 green onions, chopped

1 cup raw peanuts, lightly browned in oil, crushed

Chopped fresh coriander

In a bowl, pour boiling water over noodles. Soak until just soft, about 20 minutes; drain. Combine fish sauce, sugar, vinegar, soy sauce, oyster sauce and ketchup; toss 1 tbsp. sauce with noodles. In a skillet over medium heat, heat oil; fry onion, ginger and garlic briefly. Toss in chicken and shrimp, cooking about 5 minutes. Toss in chili paste; cook another 2 minutes. Stir in remaining fish sauce mix; cook a further 1 to 2 minutes. Gently fold in noodles to heat. Move to one side of pan, and pour in eggs, gently stirring until just set. Combine with noodles and spoon onto large platter. Surround with sprouts. Garnish with lime wedges. Sprinkle on green onions, peanuts and a scattering of coriander. Serves 6.

COUSCOUS

COMMONLY THOUGHT OF AS A GRAIN, COUSCOUS IS MADE from durum-wheat semolina and is more correctly a pasta. It is fast-cooking and the basis of some of the best and simplest cooking anywhere—and in all its variety provides the great dishes of the Maghreb (Morocco, Algeria, Tunisia, plus, some would say, southern Spain, still greatly influenced by its Moorish centuries). Yet in North America it remains marginal, enjoyed mainly in homes that grew up with it and those eating places that do wondrous things with grated carrot, a few raisins and a couple of sticks of celery. Couscous deserves better.

Its origins are murky but are generally credited to the Berbers, the ferociously individualistic (if you were a Berber; bloody-minded rebels if you were not) Caucasoid nomads of North Africa. There the word is used variously for the pre-pared food, the pot it is cooked in and the ingredient itself—semolina, made from hard wheat, moistened with water, flour-coated, then rubbed by hand (in the Maghreb) into tiny pellets. Most of the rest of the world, in its endless quest for more time it doesn't know what to do with, uses commercial brands. Like commercial noodles, it is perfectly good and generally comes in three calibers: fine, medium, coarse.

The cooking (steaming, not boiling) is best done in a couscoussier. This is a two-part vessel: deep stock pot, per-forated steamer. Below, the tagine (stew) of main ingredients (fish, meat, vegetables, whatever comes to the inventive mind) simmering nicely; between top and bottom, a fine piece of cheesecloth; above, the couscous pellets cooking in the richly flavored steam.

How richly? Spices common to Mediterranean cous-cous: cinnamon, cumin, cloves, aniseed, saffron, sesame seeds, ginger, black and cayenne peppers. If that's not pun-gent enough, consider a side dish of *harissa*, the aromatically fierce North African hot sauce made of cayenne, coriander, garlic, mint and olive oil.

For the Maghrebi the result is a staple; also a must for Jews as well as Muslims at celebrations, not least on the sabbath. For the rest of us, still exploring the closer boundaries of Italian pasta, couscous remains on the starting blocks, waiting for the bang.

Couscous PILAF

1 onion, finely chopped (3/4 cup)

1 clove garlic, minced

1 stalk celery, finely chopped (1/2 cup)

1 carrot, finely chopped (1/2 cup)

2 tbsp. olive oil

2 tbsp. butter

2 cups couscous

2 1/2 cups chicken stock

1 bay leaf

In a large saucepan over medium heat, soften onion, garlic, celery and carrot in hot oil and butter. Stir in couscous; cook until lightly browned. Add stock and bay leaf; bring to a boil. Remove from heat, cover and let stand 15 minutes. Fluff with fork. Discard bay leaf. Serves 4.

RICE

RICE IS NOW GROWN AROUND THE GLOBE, IN PLACES WITH unrationed supplies of water, heat and mosquitoes. It seems to have originated in southern India, and for most of Asia it has been a staple since about 3000 BC (though Japan was a latecomer). It took 4,000 years or so to get to Europe in a big way—courtesy of the marauding Moors—and then needed several more centuries before it took hold in the Caribbean, Central and South America and eventually Australia.

It arrived in North America by happy accident. In 1671 a sea captain was shipwrecked on the coast of the British colony of South Carolina. His vessel patched up, the grateful skipper gave a bag of Madagascar seed rice to Dr. Henry Woodward of Charleston—the foundation of the future state's ante-bellum riches. Today rice flourishes in Florida, Louisiana, Mississippi, Arkansas, Texas and California (but no longer, curiously, in South Carolina). The result is that the United States is now the world's sixth-largest producer of rice, and for 25 years its leading exporter.

This despite the fact that 90 percent of the world's rice is grown in Asia. The reasons are twofold: Asians eat even more than they produce, Americans infinitely less. The Chinese scarf down about 360 lb. of rice per year apiece, the Japanese about 180 lb., Americans—and Canadians, who grow a delicious and expensive aquatic oat called wild rice, not technically rice at all—about 8 lb.

Further, the Burmese, for instance, obtain 70 percent of their daily calories from rice, the Japanese about 45 percent. For North Americans the figure is eight-tenths of 1 percent—but then we have never believed, with the Thais, that the human body was made of rice and therefore needed constant rice refueling to keep it working.

Our Favorite Rice
One foolproof method for long-grain white rice: No precise measurements are needed. Bring 5 or 6 cups water per cup of rice to boil, add 1 tsp. salt, stir once to ensure rice isn't sticking to bottom of pan, lower heat to medium and let the rice expand gently to its heart's content, uncovered. Set timer for 14 minutes (for white rice). When timer reaches its little epiphany, test a few grains. If still too firm, leave a minute longer. Drain thoroughly (there go the nutrients, but it tastes better). Spread into a shallow, warm bowl. Fluff gently.

Instead we have tended to agree, if not in so many words, with Sir William Crookes, president of the British Association for the Advancement of Science, who in 1898 pronounced that "civilized mankind has set wheat apart as the proper food for the development of muscle and brains." And little by little over the last 35 years the consumption of wheat in the Orient has been rising, at the expense of rice, specifically in Taiwan, South Korea and Japan. Industrialists, apparently swallowing Sir William's century-old dictum as a whole food, have determined that they could expect greater productivity from wheat-eaters than they could from those devoted to the glories of rice.

This hardly explains the continued exceptional output of those three countries where, despite the inroads of wheat and quarter-pounders, rice is still consumed by seven out of 10 of the population.

In truth, a grain of rice is a splendid storehouse of protein, fat, starch, sugar, minerals, vitamin Bs and fiber. The trouble is that by the time it reaches the market, particularly your neighborhood North American one, milling and polishing have reduced its food value considerably. And too often when we cook it we overdo it, so that it ends up on the plate as a tasteless, pasty gloop with no further purpose in life than to fill 'er up.

Short-sighted. Rice remains one of the world's few low-cost, nourishing (despite the production sins) and thoroughly digestible foods when cooked—and bought—with a little care and imagination. It would make sense to use more of both.

Cooking it: Confucius was devoted to good cooking. In his *Analects* (about 500 BC) he declared that food should not be eaten stale, or without taste, or improperly blended. Aces so far; stuff that no doubt needed to be said at the time. But Confucius, he also said that rice should be polished white.

This injunction was not widely followed, and just as well: those who did observe it and whose diet was almost exclusively rice tended to die unpleasantly of beri-beri (symptoms: fainting, progressive loss of power leading to paralysis and, alarmingly, no warning fever). Polished rice becomes lethal only when unaccompanied indefinitely by anything else, such as legumes or fish.

• Rice triples in volume (rough rule of Epicurean thumb, hereinafter termed an Analect) when cooked. Thus, 1 cup raw rice makes 3 cups cooked; allow 1 cup cooked rice per serving.

• Vigorous stirring while the rice is cooking breaks the grain and makes it sticky. Fluff gently with a fork instead.

• The reason for excessive milling is that it makes rice white, as Confucius observed; if whiteness is what you're after—hiding the evidence—a few drops of lemon juice in the cooking water will whiten less-milled rice effectively.

• Some grow dispirited with rice cooking for no other reason than they're using the wrong pot. Always use a good-sized one with a heavy bottom.

Buying it: The International Rice Research Institute has collected more than 30,000 varieties—many rice-growing communities have different hybrids not merely from paddy to paddy but within the paddy. Mercifully, the 30,000 may be broken down for brevity's sake into two main categories:

Long-grain, which cooks quite dry and is excellent for pilafs, stuffings, salads, casseroles; and short-grain, which cooks moister and stickier, and is used in puddings and sushi.

However, certain subsections, created by modern technology, create occasional confusion. In brief:

• *Instant* needs no cooking—merely mix with boiling water and let stand, covered, about 5 minutes. A typical by-product of our indigestible quest for speed, it is amorphously bland, and it should not detain us. Even 5 minutes.

• *Converted* is parboiled, steamed, dried and milled in a process that allows retention of more nutrients than

• *Polished*, which has been removed of all its outer coverings. With them go much (but not all) of its food value.

• *Brown* is unpolished rice. Only the husk has been removed. High in nutrients, slow in cooking time.

• *Arborio* (or Italian), the classic short-grain rice for risotto, is polished.

• *Basmati*, a long-grain rice that grows in the foothills of the Himalayas, has exceptional flavor and aroma; it must be washed before cooking. Carolina rice, a brand and no longer a district, is a good substitute.

RISOTTO CON GAMBERETTI
(RISOTTO WITH SHRIMP)

A risotto is a way of cooking rice, pioneered in northern Italy. Once a cook has mastered the method, any number of variations and combinations of flavors is possible. The best rice to use is the short-grained, top-quality Arborio rice grown in the Po Valley. A risotto is moist, but the cooked rice should still be al dente—a little firm and chewy. Hot broth is added a half cup at a time, until rice is cooked to a creamy consistency yet the grains are still distinct. More liquid is added only when what's already in the pot has been absorbed. For the classic risotto à la Milanese, a pinch of saffron threads is added to the broth, and extra butter and freshly grated Parmesan cheese are stirred into the rice before serving.

6 tbsp. olive oil

1 tsp. finely chopped garlic

3 tbsp. finely chopped Italian parsley

1 lb. medium shrimp, shelled and deveined

Salt and freshly ground pepper

1/2 cup dry white wine

2 1/2 to 3 cups chicken or fish stock

3 tbsp. butter

1/4 cup finely chopped onion

1 1/2 cups Arborio rice

Chopped fresh parsley

Heat 3 tbsp. oil in a large saucepan. Add garlic and parsley; cook for 2 to 3 minutes. Toss in shrimp; season with salt and pepper. Cook 2 minutes. Add wine. Simmer shrimp 5 minutes. Transfer shrimp with a slotted spoon to a bowl; set aside. Add stock to pan and bring to a simmer. In another large saucepan or casserole over medium heat, heat remaining oil and 2 tbsp. butter. Add onion; cook until soft but not brown. Stir in rice; cook 3 to 4 minutes. Slowly add 1/2 cup hot broth; stir gently while liquid is absorbed. Keep rice moist by adding

more broth, 1/2 cup at a time, stirring lightly. Towards the end of the cooking time (about 20 to 30 minutes), add liquid 1 or 2 tbsp. at a time. The cooked rice should be al dente and all liquid should have been absorbed. Adjust seasoning. Add shrimp to rice in pan, toss with remaining butter and parsley, and dish out at once.
Serves 4.

*P*ILAF WITH WHOLE SPICES

The Punjabis brought this dish to perfection. The spices are left whole as a decoration and are not eaten (although if bitten into, they would not be harmful).

3 tbsp. light vegetable oil or clarified butter (ghee)

1 medium onion, finely chopped

1 clove garlic, chopped

1 tsp. cumin seeds

6 small cardamom pods

1 cinnamon stick

4 cloves

2 bay leaves

6 whole black peppercorns

2 cups basmati rice (*see below*)

4 cups water (use basmati soaking water)

1 tsp. salt

Onion slices browned in butter until crisp, for garnish

Heat oil in a large heavy saucepan over medium heat; gently cook onion until softened. Add garlic; cook a minute or so. Stir in spices; cook less than a minute, or until seeds and pods are puffed and fragrant. Add rice; stir to coat with spicy mixture 2 to 3 minutes. Add water and salt; stir gently while water comes to a boil. Cook, loosely covered, over low heat 10 minutes. Turn heat to lowest setting, cover pot tightly and steam 10 minutes. Turn off heat, and let rest undisturbed 5 minutes. Fluff gently before serving. Place in a shallow, warm bowl, and garnish with browned onion slices.
Serves 6 to 8.

To prepare basmati rice: Pick out any debris, and put rice in a large bowl. Cover with cold water. After rice settles on bottom, pour off water. Repeat once or twice until water runs clear. Drain rice, then cover with twice its amount in fresh cold water. Soak 30 minutes. (In Indian cooking, rice is cooked in the water in which it soaked.)

ORIENTAL RICE SALAD

2 cups cooked brown rice

1/2 cup toasted salted cashews

1/2 cup raisins

1/2 cup water chestnuts, drained and sliced

1 sweet green pepper, seeded and chopped

3 green onions, cut diagonally

2 stalks celery, cut diagonally

Fresh parsley, chopped

1 clove garlic, finely chopped

1 tsp. grated fresh ginger

1/4 tsp. salt

Freshly ground pepper

2 tbsp. rice vinegar

Juice of 1 lemon

1 tsp. sugar

4 tbsp. soy sauce

1/4 cup peanut oil

1 tbsp. sesame oil

1/4 cup toasted sesame seeds

As Louis Armstrong used to end his letters: "Red beans and ricely yours, Satch."

In a large bowl combine brown rice with cashews, raisins, water chestnuts, green pepper, green onions, celery and parsley. In a small bowl, mash together garlic, ginger, salt and pepper. Add vinegar, lemon juice, sugar and soy sauce; whisk in oils. Toss rice mixture with dressing. Chill until ready to serve.
Serves 4 to 6.

Fowl

CHICKEN

OUR CHICKEN CONSUMPTION HAS TRIPLED IN THE PAST 30 years, and it's not hard to see why. Once the conscience has eased itself past considering the battery-reared chicken's insomniac, one-foot-square, seven-week life, we find it repays us in degrees of taste and nutrition in direct proportional contrast to its miserable existence. Its meat is a high-quality protein, a good source of niacin and iron; it is endlessly economical through boom or bust (one generous half-pound serving costs less than $2; is readily digestible by the toothless young or crapulous old; and has a low-fat content—particularly if prepared skinless—and a high one of linoleic acid (which as every schoolchild knows, can be translated as $C_{18}H_{32}O_2$, and is thought to lower cholesterol levels).

The chicken originated the usual millennia ago in the Malaysian jungle, was first domesticated in the Indus river valley, and finally made it to the West, specifically Greece, some time in the fifth century BC. Perhaps because there has always been something vaguely absurd about it, the chicken was never deified in the way other fowl, such as turkey, goose, duck and swan, have managed in various jurisdictions throughout their long histories. The ancient Egyptians, who deified almost anything with a pulse, never got around to the chicken because they had no chickens in the first place. Nobody has bothered to investigate the chicken's language, in the way the great naturalist Konrad Lorenz investigated—and mastered—the language of geese. The chicken, poor soul, has had to make do with massive ritual secular martyrdom on the altar of the world's tables, a culinary sacrifice that expands in scope with each passing year.

Still, the male of the species does have its name recorded by the ancient Greeks as a fitting tribute to Asclepius, god of medicine. Thus the last words of Socrates, rather too late—or was it Socratic irony?—after drinking hemlock: "Crito, we ought to offer a cock to Asclepius. See to it, and don't forget." If only he'd thought of it earlier.

CHICKEN WITH CITRUS SAUCE AND GLAZED ZEST

3 whole boneless, skinned chicken breasts, split
Salt and freshly ground pepper
1 tbsp. olive oil
1 to 2 tbsp. butter
3 shallots or green onions, chopped
1 tbsp. lemon juice
2 tbsp. orange juice
1/4 cup dry white wine
1 cup chicken stock
1/2 tsp. dried thyme
Glazed Citrus Zest (*recipe follows*)

Lightly season chicken with salt and pepper. Heat oil and butter in a large skillet over medium-high heat. Add chicken and brown well on all sides. Lift from pan and set aside. Pour away most of the fat. Add shallots; sauté to soften. Whisk in juices, wine and stock; bring just to a boil. Return chicken to pan; sprinkle thyme on top; lower heat and cook, covered, about 15 minutes. Transfer chicken pieces to a warm platter. Toss in Glazed Citrus Zest. Increase heat and reduce pan juices briskly until lightly thickened; adjust seasoning. Spoon over chicken. Garnish with finely chopped parsley.
Serves 4.

Glazed Citrus Zest

1 lemon

1 orange

2 tbsp. sugar

4 tbsp. reserved water

1 tbsp. butter

Scrub fruit under warm water; dry well. With a sharp knife, peel zest (skin only, not bitter white pith) and slice in thin strips. Blanch in boiling water 2 minutes; drain, reserving juice. Return to pot with sugar, water and butter. Toss and cook over medium heat until nicely glazed, approximately 5 minutes.

CHICKEN-SHALLOT FRICASSEE

An unusual aromatic version of a simple chicken braise.

6 chicken pieces

Freshly ground pepper

1 tsp. paprika

2 tbsp. fruity olive oil

1 tbsp. butter

1/2 cup each finely chopped onion, carrot, celery stalk

1/2 cup dry vermouth

1 tbsp. chopped fresh tarragon

1 tsp. grated lemon rind

Glazed Shallots (*recipe follows*)

1/4 cup 35% cream (optional)

Rub chicken well with pepper and lightly dust with paprika. In a large skillet, heat oil and butter; sauté chicken until well browned. Remove and set aside. Drain off all but 2 tbsp. fat. Add onion, carrot and celery; cook slowly until softened. Increase heat. Add vermouth; reduce briskly by half. Return chicken to pan along with tarragon and lemon rind. Simmer, partially covered, until cooked through, about 25 minutes. Toss in shallots; bring briskly to a boil; lower heat and cook gently for 5 minutes to meld flavors. Transfer the whole lot to a large warm platter. Return skillet to the heat; swirl in cream and boil briefly, stirring, to reduce and lightly thicken. Spoon onto chicken. Garnish with additional tarragon. Serve with basmati rice or steamed couscous. Serves 4 to 6.

Glazed Shallots
1/2 lb. shallots (16)
2 tbsp. butter
1 tsp. sugar

Snip root end of shallots; peel. Cook shallots gently in butter for 5 minutes. Sprinkle with sugar. Toss to coat well. Cook, covered, until tender and nicely glazed, 10 to 15 minutes.

GRILLED ASIAN CHICKEN

Coconut milk ensures a juicy, moist bird. (Pictured opposite page 88.)
1 whole roasting chicken (2 1/2 lb.)
1 small onion, finely chopped
2 cloves garlic, minced
1 tsp. grated fresh ginger,
1 tsp. coarsely ground black pepper
3 small chilies, minced or 2 tsp. hot chili paste
1 tsp. ground turmeric
1 stalk lemongrass, chopped, white part only
1 cup coconut milk

Turn chicken, breast side down. Using kitchen shears, cut along both sides of backbone all the way through lengthwise. Discard backbone. Turn chicken over and push hard on breastbone to flatten. Bend the legs inward. Insert a wooden skewer through the base of the legs and the tail to hold them firmly together. Mix onion, garlic, ginger, pepper, chilies, turmeric and lemongrass to a fine paste. (A food processor does an admirable job.) Rub chicken with this mixture and let stand 2 hours or overnight refrigerated. Place coconut milk in a large skillet. Add chicken and partially cover; simmer gently (do not boil) until just tender, turning once. Remove from sauce, pat dry and grill over a low charcoal fire or under the broiler about 10 to 15 minutes, until crispy brown and lightly charred. Serve with deep-fried shrimp chips, basmati rice and Mango Salsa (p. 144).
Serves 4 to 6.

Tip: 1 tbsp. grated lemon rind may be substituted for the lemongrass.

THAI ROAST CHICKEN

A chicken stuffed with all manner of herbs and seasonings is a wondrous thing. This is a particularly succulent Oriental version.

1 or 2 stalks lemongrass, white part only

4 slices fresh ginger, peeled

1 roasting chicken (3 to 5 lb.)

8 cloves garlic, halved

1 small onion, peeled and quartered

1/2 lemon, sliced

A large handful of fresh herbs (tarragon, rosemary, thyme, oregano)

2 bay leaves

1 tsp. paprika

2 tbsp. softened butter

Fowls are to the kitchen what the canvas is to the painter.
—Jean-Anthelme Brillat-Savarin

Smash lemongrass and ginger with flat side of a heavy knife to release flavors. Stuff chicken with lemongrass, ginger, garlic, onion, lemon slices and herbs. Truss. Rub skin with paprika and softened butter. Roast at 325°F for 1 1/2 hours (25 minutes per lb.) or until legs wiggle and juices run clear when skin is pricked. Remove chicken to platter and keep warm. (Drain fat, add 1/4 cup frozen orange juice concentrate and 1 cup chicken stock. Boil briskly, stirring until slightly reduced.)
Serves 4 to 8.

ROAST CAPON WITH MUSHROOM AND WALNUT STUFFING

A fine roast capon provides a large amount of tender, lean meat and a particularly welcome treat for palates weary or wary of beef. Remember, when roasting a whole bird: truss the wings and legs securely to the bird. This makes handling during cooking much easier.

1 capon (around 6 lb.)
Mushroom and Walnut Stuffing (*recipe follows*)
1 tbsp. butter, softened
1 each onion, carrot, celery stalk and parsnip, coarsely chopped
1 bay leaf
1 clove garlic
1 cup chicken stock (or 1/2 cup wine, 1/2 cup stock)

Clean capon carefully, season neck and body cavities with salt and pepper, stuff loosely and truss securely. Rub a roasting pan and the bird with a little soft butter; set the capon, breast up, in the pan and scatter around chopped vegetables, the neck, gizzard and heart of the capon, bay leaf and garlic. Bake at 425°F. After 15 minutes, baste and turn the capon on its side. After 15 more minutes, baste and turn the bird on the other side. Fifteen minutes later still, set the bird breast up, baste and cover loosely with a sheet of foil; lower the heat to 375°F and continue roasting, basting often. After about an hour remove the foil, depending on the brownness; continue basting and roasting until the meat is tender and the juices run clear (allow about 20 minutes per pound.) Transfer capon to a warm platter. Pour the fat from the roasting pan; add chicken stock. Bring to a vigorous boil, scraping up the accumulated juices; strain, pressing down on the vegetables to release their goodness. Adjust seasoning. If necessary, return the sauce to the heat in a small saucepan and reduce. Glaze the capon with a few spoonfuls of sauce and serve the rest separately. Less trouble than it sounds; or, looked at another way, more than worth the trouble it takes.

Serves 6.

Mushroom and Walnut Stuffing

1/2 cup walnuts

1/2 lb. sausage meat

2 tbsp. butter

1/2 tsp. dried thyme

1/2 cup finely chopped onions

1/4 cup chopped parsley

1/4 lb. wild mushrooms, cleaned and chopped

Salt and freshly ground pepper

1 clove garlic, minced

2 cups fresh white bread crumbs

The liver from the capon, chopped

1 egg, lightly beaten

Toast walnuts on a baking sheet 400°F for 5 minutes until crisp. Chop coarsely; set aside. Melt butter in a heavy skillet over medium heat. Add onions; cook until soft. Add mushrooms and garlic. Raise heat to moderate and stir and cook until mushroom liquid evaporates. Add chopped liver; toss until softened. Add sausage meat, breaking it up and cooking until lightly browned. Remove pan from heat, blend in herbs, seasonings, bread crumbs, egg and walnuts. Cool.

CHICKEN PAPRIKASH

The secret to this classic Hungarian version is: don't try to economize by cutting back on the onions. They reduce to a rich, redolent sauce.

4 tbsp. butter

6 large cooking onions, chopped (3 1/2 cups)

1/2 tsp. salt

4 cloves garlic, chopped

2 sweet green peppers, seeded and chopped

4 or 5 whole boneless, skinned chicken breasts, trimmed
   and halved

Freshly ground white pepper

4 tbsp. all-purpose flour

2 cups chicken stock

2 cups sour cream

2 tbsp. sweet paprika

Melt butter in a large skillet over very low heat. Sauté onions with salt until golden. Toss in garlic and green peppers. Cook briefly. Spread chicken on top of onion mixture. Simmer, covered, over medium-low heat for 5 to 7 minutes. Uncover and lightly pepper chicken pieces before turning them over. Cover, return to simmer for another 5 to 7 minutes. Transfer chicken to a plate and set aside. Stir flour into onion mixture; cook 2 minutes. Swirl in chicken stock and sour cream. Blend in paprika and let thicken. Return chicken pieces to pan and cover them with sauce; heat through. (Recipe can be made ahead to this point; it will keep for a day or two in the fridge. Reheat for 30 minutes over low heat, or carefully transfer chicken paprikash into an ovenproof serving dish and reheat at 350°F for up to 30 minutes, until piping hot.) Serve with homemade Spätzle (recipe follows).
Serves 8 to 10.

Spätzle

A spätzle maker is available at kitchen supply stores.

3 cups all-purpose flour

1/2 tsp. salt

1 tsp. freshly ground nutmeg, or more

3 large eggs, lightly beaten

3/4 cup milk

1/4 to 1/2 cup chicken broth

1 tbsp. butter

1/4 cup chopped parsley

Bring a large pot of salted water to a rolling boil. While it heats up, mix together flour, salt and nutmeg. Beat in eggs. Gradually beat in milk and broth, beating till mixture forms a smooth dough. Pass dough through a spätzle maker into boiling water, forming short, shred-like noodles. Immediately remove and drain; rinse with cold water. Before serving, sauté spätzle briefly in butter, season to taste with a bit more salt and sprinkle with chopped parsley.

Tip: If you don't have a spätzle maker, push the dough through the wide holes of a colander—a messy business but quite effective.

CRYSTAL FOLD

This may seem a bit of a bore: too much chopping, slicing, dicing.
Bear with us and you will find it becomes standard fare.

1/4 cup Japanese soy sauce

1 tbsp. sesame oil

1 tbsp. cornstarch

2 green onions

2-inch piece fresh ginger, peeled and sliced

2 cloves garlic, halved

2 lb. boneless chicken breast or pork tenderloin,
   cut in thin strips

3 tbsp. peanut oil

1 cup julienned carrot, 2-inch strips

1 cup julienned celery, 2-inch strips

1 cup julienned green onion, 2-inch strips

4 oz. rice sticks

Peanut oil for deep-frying

1/4 cup hoisin sauce

12 iceberg lettuce leaves

Louis, Marquis de Cussy (1766–1837), one of Napoleon's top aides, is said to have invented 366 different ways to cook chicken: one for each day, not forgetting leap year. Alas, none seem to have survived (very long after) Waterloo.

Blend together well soy sauce, sesame oil and cornstarch. Discard tops of green onion, halve and slice in thin strips. Add to soy base along with ginger, garlic and chicken. Refrigerate, covered, for 1 hour; drain. In a wok or large, heavy skillet over high heat, stir-fry ginger, garlic and chicken in hot oil, a handful at a time, until just cooked through. Transfer chicken to a dish and set aside. Add vegetables to pan. Toss and cook until softened, adding more oil if necessary. Return chicken to pan and heat through. Discard garlic and ginger chunks. Break rice sticks into 4-inch lengths. Deep-fry a handful at a time in 2 inches of oil until they puff up (this will take only a few seconds per batch). Drain well on paper towels. To serve, each person spreads a little hoisin sauce on a lettuce leaf and tops it with deep-fried noodles, then the chicken mixture. Finally, wrap the whole lot up taco-style. Now try to eat it. Serves 6.

DRUNKEN CHICKEN SALAD

Drunken chicken is a Chinese method of poaching whole chicken: a splendidly delicate base for a salad. Our version is simplified by using boneless chicken breasts.

1/4 cup sherry

2 slices fresh ginger, peeled

1 green onion, roughly chopped

2 cups chicken stock

4 boneless, skinless chicken breasts

1 tbsp. lemon juice

3 tbsp. olive oil

1 tsp. Dijon mustard

1/4 tsp. salt

Freshly ground pepper

1/2 cup toasted cashews

2 cups bean sprouts

2 bunches watercress

4 Boston lettuce leaves

"There's cold chicken inside it," replied the Rat briefly; "coldtonguecoldhamcoldbeefpickledgherkinssaladfrenchrollscresssandwichespottedmeatgingerbeerlemonadesodawater—"
"O stop, stop," cried the Mole in ecstasies: "This is too much!"
—Kenneth Grahame, The Wind in the Willows.

Combine sherry, ginger, green onion and stock in a medium saucepan. Bring to a boil. Slip in chicken breasts and simmer very gently until just tender. Let cool in cooking liquid. Drain chicken; cut into strips. (The leftover broth makes a wonderfully light soup.) Combine lemon juice, oil, mustard, salt and pepper; whisk until creamy.
Toss together chicken, cashews, bean sprouts, watercress and dressing. Eat cold in lettuce cups.
Serves 4.

DUCK

THE DUCK, FOR WHOM POULTRY YARDS WERE INVENTED, has a noble international history. The Sumerians deemed the wild version worthy of the gods 3,000 years before Christ, the Egyptians fed it to Pharaohs, the Maya fed it to themselves while pioneering double-decimal mathematics centuries before the arrival of the Spanish conquistadores (greater experts in decimation). The Chinese, who domesticated it four millennia ago, have never lost their reverence for it: many Sinophiles maintain that the ultimate Chinese duck dish is the one called the Seventeen Ineffable Precious Parts of the Duck, which gives some idea of the esteem in which the Chinese hold it.

The only duck most of us will ever eat is our domestic Pekin duck, a descendant of the wild mallard—though here and there (mostly there) may be found a farmer raising the gamier Muscovy strain popular from Mexico to southern Brazil.

The Long Island ducklings so often found on menus whose reach exceeds their grasp are no different from the ones raised in, let's say, Quebec or Oregon. Indeed, they may well have been raised there: no one would know the difference since all would be Pekin, thanks to one Major Ashley, a British army officer stationed in Peking in the 1870s, who set about raising a few Chinese ducks for his own purposes. In 1873 an American clipper dropped by, with a Yankee trader named James Palmer aboard. Palmer persuaded Ashley to part with a few of his ducks and their offspring are what we're dealing with now.

After a short digression.

Only one of us has eaten pressed duck, though we have all seen the odd duck press gathering dust on a restaurant sideboard. We harbor a suspicion—a wish, even—that some bright restaurateur may soon open a place that puts all these old contraptions, as quirkily particular as samovars, to gainful employment, serving nothing *but* pressed duck.

What makes pressed duck different is that it dies by strangulation, not the knife, and the carcass, meaty part removed, is pressed to make a sauce largely of its own blood, thickened with port and cognac and its own chopped-up liver. Plainly it is not an easy dish to prepare: aside from the expensive press, it requires a large and fresh supply of ducks, since unbled ducks, left lying around, are soon prone to infection.

The ultimate in pressed duck, also known as *canard au sang* and *canard à la rouennaise,* is probably to be found at La Couronne in Rouen, a restaurant built in 1345 on the square where, 86 years later, Joan of Arc was burned at the stake; and at the Tour d'Argent, Paris's oldest restaurant (1582), which looks onto the Seine and Notre Dame. Since 1890 this latter citadel of Michelin three-star French cooking has kept a record of every pressed duck it has served. The first book has been lost, unfortunately, so nobody knows who ordered Number 1. But we do know that Edward VII, as Prince of Wales, had Number 328; Theodore Roosevelt Number 33,642; the Duke of Windsor, 147,888; his niece Elizabeth and the Duke of Edinburgh, Numbers 185,397 and 185,398 (in 1948); Charlie Chaplin, Number 253,652. In 1984 the number passed 640,000; now it is more than 800,000 and should reach the million mark by the millennium.

Serve a duck whole, but eat only the breast and neck. The rest send back to the cook.
—Martial (40–102), Roman epigrammist.

CHINESE-STYLE ROASTED DUCK

A pungent, elutriative variant, and simple to boot. (Pictured opposite page 89.)

3 tbsp. soy sauce

3 tbsp. dry sherry

3 green onions, chopped

2 cloves garlic, peeled and mashed

1 duckling (4 to 5 lb.)

Rind of 2 oranges, cut in slivers

1 slice fresh ginger, peeled

2 tbsp. liquid honey

Juice of 1/2 orange (1/4 cup)

1/2 cup hot stock or water

Wipe duck well, inside and out, with a damp cloth. Prick the skin all over to allow fat to drain from duck. Combine soy sauce, sherry, onions and garlic. Discard excess fat from the neck and cavity, tuck the orange rind and ginger into the cavity and pour in half the soy mixture. Truss the duck. Add honey to the rest of the soy mixture and rub some of it over the skin. Place duck directly on an oven rack above a large pan holding 1 or 2 inches of water; or secure it on a rôtisserie. Roast at 325°F. Add orange juice and hot stock to remaining soy mixture and baste duck frequently until the meat is tender and skin a glorious dark brown, about 2 to 3 hours.
A feast for 2, enough for 3.

Meats

BEEF

BEEF—"THE SOUL OF COOKING," CROONED ANTONIN Carème, the storied nineteenth-century French chef—has been having a hard time of it, taking it in the chops from every side: price, health, ecology, a troika that must make beef's ad agencies demand triple time and danger pay. On the other side of the ring, wearing a watchful look and a constant tic, stands the chicken, perceived as offering better odds in all three areas.

Small wonder, then, that North American beef consumption has been sinking like a punctured balloon, by well over 20 percent between 1974 and 1993: from 85 to 65 lbs. per person per year in the U.S., 95 to 70 lbs. in Canada. In the same period, borne by the heady thermals of low cost and New Nutrition, chicken has taken off in the U.S. from about 40 lbs. per person/year 20 years ago to 72 lbs. today—an 80 percent increase—in Canada, from 30 to 51 lbs.

The favorite argument of vegetarian ecologists is that if everyone ate as much beef as North Americans, they couldn't. The reason: it's supposed to take two acres of land per person to raise the amount of beef we still eat, and there's less than one acre of arable land per person in the world. Underlying this argument runs the accusatory subtext that Americans and Canadians are the world's biggest beef eaters and should therefore spend the rest of our days in atonement, eating sunflower seeds. In fact, Argentinians and Uruguayans, per capita, beat North Americans hollow.

What also gets lost in this thesis is that beef is still a fine source of protein, and that its proteins are much more thoroughly and efficiently utilized by the human digestive tract than those ingested through a vegetarian diet. Trimmed of fat, taken in reasonable quantities, beef is good for us, rich in iron and the B vitamins.

Heaven sends us good meat, but the Devil sends us cooks.
—David Garrick, actor-poet (1717–1779).

There are those, leaning on the testosterone button and doubtless steroid abusers to boot, who argue that meat eating is necessary to build mental sinew, too; that only carnivores can hope to score knockouts in the ring of life. From this it apparently follows that a regular intake of sirloin is required to win wars—and therefore also to start them. Would the equation were that simple! Then we could get rid of all our shorthorns and charolais, wiping out in one swell foop 8,000 years of domestication on one hand and all armed conflicts on the other. Peace in our bean-sprouts-and-tofu time!

But where does this leave the gentle Inuit, otherwise known, and quite legitimately, as the Eskimo? They eat huge quantities of red meat, much of it raw. Yet they are a peaceable people, happy enough not to be spending their time thinking up new ways to change the course of history. (Apropos names: Eskimo is derived from what Algonquians called them and means eater of raw meat.)

Raw, rare, medium if you must, beef offers lasting pleasures and benefits denied the strict vegetarian, for all that abstaining from flesh has had overtones of virtue and sexless purity for centuries. God Almighty first planted a garden, true enough, but if he'd meant us to live on botany, would He have given us canines and incisors? So let us change the course of history on our own terms.

GRILLED TENDERLOIN

Beef tenderloin is at its best well-marinated, simply grilled or roasted, and then thinly sliced.

1 tbsp. crushed peppercorns

2 cloves garlic, halved

1 small onion, chopped

1 bay leaf

2 shallots, chopped

4 tbsp. balsamic vinegar

1/2 cup olive oil

1 tsp. Dijon mustard

1 beef tenderloin (2 lb.)

Aglais, a Greek actress in third-century Rome, thought nothing of eating 10 lb. of beef at a sitting, helpfully easing it down with half a dozen jugs of wine.

Rub beef well with peppercorns. Combine garlic, onion, bay leaf, shallots, vinegar, oil and mustard. Add beef to marinade and turn (to coat well). Let stand 2 hours. Sear over hot coals, then barbecue on indirect heat—with top down—or roast in a 450°F oven approximately 20 minutes per lb. for rare. Let rest 15 minutes before slicing thinly to serve.

Serves 6.

THE ULTIMATE BURGER

Simpler than it sounds, this is our burger benchmark. A well-seasoned cast-iron skillet is the best to use, better in this instance than the barbecue.

1 lb. sirloin tip (fast-fry steaks are perfect since they
  are already thinly sliced)
3 tbsp. very finely chopped onion
Salt and freshly ground pepper
2 tsp. balsamic or red wine vinegar
2 tbsp. butter
2 tbsp. olive oil
Buns, crusty on the outside and soft on the inside
Crispy Onions (*recipe follows*)

Using a very sharp cleaver or chef's knife, cut meat into thin strips, then into tiny cubes. Keep chopping the whole lot as you would parsley. Add onion and continue chopping until a firm mince is obtained. Add salt and pepper and drizzle with balsamic vinegar. Carefully shape the meat together into four patties. Press lightly just to hold together, rather like handling pastry. Sauté ever so gently in butter and oil until just cooked through; a raw center is not desirable for flavor unless that is your fancy. Lightly toast the bun and drizzle with a little of the beef juices. Top with the burger and spoon on a little extra juice. Pile on crispy onions. Bring on the ice-cold beer and the hammock.
Makes 4.

Crispy Onions
1 Spanish onion, very thinly sliced
2 tbsp. butter
1 tbsp. olive oil
1/2 tsp. sugar

In a cast-iron skillet, cook onions over medium-high heat in butter and olive oil. Stir frequently until lightly browned. Sprinkle with sugar; continue cooking until crisp and well browned.

VEAL WITH PUTTANESCA SAUCE

Veal comes to life with the sauce made famous by Roman strumpets.

4 veal loin chops, 1 inch thick

3 tbsp. olive oil

1 onion, sliced

4 to 6 cloves garlic, minced

2 cups canned plum tomatoes, drained, seeded and chopped

1/2 cup pitted, chopped ripe olives

1/4 cup capers, drained

1 tsp. dried oregano

1 tsp. dried basil

Pinch hot pepper flakes

Dash lemon juice or balsamic vinegar

Freshly ground pepper

In a heavy skillet, brown chops lightly on both sides in oil; remove and set aside. In same pan cook onion and garlic until softened. Stir in remaining ingredients, return chops, and simmer, covered, about 35 minutes. Adjust seasoning. Accompany with pasta or crisp oven-roasted potatoes.
Serves 4.

LIVER

C AN IT BE THAT LIVER, SO LONG REVILED, SO OFTEN infamously prepared, is enjoying a resurgence? Supplying the reinforcements for sweetbreads, the lonely frontline in offal's rearguard battle for the American table? As a starter, mushed up with cream and spices and a shot or two of brandy, livers from various sources, especially when frenchified as *foie*, have long been okay; but as a main course? Forget it.

Empirical evidence suggests this is changing, and liver (veal and beef) is starting to show up, with increasing confidence, on menus in and out of the home. And high time, too. For millennia, the liver, which once held pride of place in entrail-readings among Etruscan and Babylonian soothsayers, has had to sit below the salt in simile and song. For just as long, the heart, the brain, the lungs have had the good press, hymned by lovers, immortalized by poets—among them Plato, who situated the big emotions (love, courage) above the diaphragm, the lesser ones (lust, sloth) below it, down *there* with the looming, lazy liver.

And so lily-livered went (and remains) unchallenged as a synonym for cowardly (with no "red-livered" invented for the brave), and bile, of which the liver produces about a pint a day, became the root term for peevish bloody-mindedness.

This despite the fact that without our daily pint of bile "we could not digest so much as a single raisin," as Richard Selzer observes in *Mortal Lessons*, his lyrically haunting studies of surgery, "and therefore we should become rather more cantankerous and grouchy than we are."

We paid no notice, and our exemplary workaday friend, our blood cleanser, a miraculously helpful and self-restorative organ given half a chance, became scarcely talked about in polite circles. (In less polite ones there was no such

compunction: the Dakota Indians, working on the theory that the liver was the seat of courage, used to eat the livers of their enemies; conversely, Jeremiah Johnson, a legendary Old West mountain man of the nineteenth century, played in the movies by Robert Redford, claimed to have eaten 247 Crow Indian livers during his lifetime.)

What was not discussed about themselves carried over as prejudice into the kitchen. Since polite circles didn't care for their own livers, they weren't about to embrace—such is the human capacity to anthropomorphize anything that flies, gambols, roots or ruminates—the livers of their feathered or four-footed friends.

And now—can it be?—all this prejudice is disappearing, like unwanted gas. Just as well: liver is stiff with iron, folate, vitamin A, and a good source of potassium and the Bs. If it has a failing, it rates high in cholesterol—but let it pass. It's not as if liver is yet on our tables *every* day.

To cook: For all its rough-and-ready history, liver is a subtle food, to be treated with respect. Overcooking denies it that, and the liver will wreak its revenge by turning tough as a topsole.

Cut out blood vessels, fat and membranes. Cook fresh liver within two days; if well wrapped and frozen, within three months.

Lamb, chicken and duck livers may be sautéed, braised or grilled. Similarly beef, after a good soaking in milk or lightly salted water for 2 to 3 hours.

Veal liver may be thinly sliced and sautéed in hot butter or olive oil for little more than the blink of an eye, the pan briefly deglazed with a little wine; or fry bacon crisp with some sliced onion, then sauté the veal liver slices on top.

FEGATO ALLA VENEZIANA
(VENETIAN CALVES' LIVER)

Venice's gift to liver lovers, for all its simplicity, is possibly the best liver dish in the world. (The liver must be sliced no more than 1/4 inch thick.)

3 tbsp. olive oil

2 tbsp. butter

4 medium onions, thinly sliced

1 1/2 lb. calves' liver, sliced 1/4-inch thick

Salt and freshly ground pepper

2 tbsp. chopped parsley

A splash of balsamic vinegar

Heat oil and 1 tbsp. butter in a large, heavy skillet. Cook onions over medium-low heat, stirring from time to time as they become sweet, tender and lightly browned, about 30 minutes. Remove onions from pan with a slotted spoon, leaving fragrant oil behind. Add remaining butter to pan and raise heat to moderate. Cook liver slices until just tender—a minute a side should be long enough. Return onions to pan; season with salt and pepper. Sprinkle with parsley and balsamic vinegar and serve at once. This dish is traditionally accompanied by lightly fried polenta slices.
Serves 4.

PORK

SO TO THE PIG. THERE'S NO SUCH THING AS A NATIVE
American porker, since the first pigs—13 of them,
cousins to the wild boar—were imported to Tampa,
Florida, some 500 years ago. Go back long enough
and we find that the Chinese domesticated the pig 3,000
years before Christ (and grew to love it so much that now it
ranks up there with the duck and the carp in their culinary
pantheon).

Today's pork—long and cruelly debased as the catchall
repository of ignorant, pearls-before-swinish, troughlike
behavior and comprehensive pigging out—remains succulently juicy, rich with B vitamins . . . yet leaner than it has ever
been. A 4-ounce serving of tenderloin contains only about
185 calories, 30 percent fewer than 15 years ago: the same as
skinless chicken breast.

PORK MEDALLIONS WITH GREEN GRAPES

Pork responds superbly to fruit. This dish may sound richly old-fashioned but it remains one of our most requested recipes.

2 lb. pork tenderloin

2 to 4 tbsp. butter

2 shallots, finely chopped

1 clove garlic, minced

1/2 tsp. dried thyme

1/4 cup dry vermouth

1/2 cup chicken stock

1 cup 35% cream

2 oranges

1 1/2 lb. seedless green grapes

Slice pork in 1/2-inch slices and flatten to form medallions. Melt 2 tbsp. butter in a large skillet over medium heat; cook medallions 2 to 3 minutes on each side or until tender. Remove to a hot platter and keep warm. Sauté shallots and garlic in the skillet until just softened, adding more butter if necessary. Stir in thyme, vermouth and chicken stock; boil until reduced by half. Whisk in cream; boil gently until lightly thickened. Remove from heat. Peel skin and white pith from oranges, and divide into sections. In another saucepan, toss oranges and grapes in a little extra butter to heat through. Stir fruit into cream sauce, heat through and pour over medallions.
Serves 4.

Variation: If 35% cream is not on your most-requested list, substitute 1/4 cup frozen orange juice concentrate for the cream. Finish with 1 or 2 tbsp. cream to smooth out the sauce.

JAMAICAN JERK PORK

This recipe is adapted from one served at Mark's Place, a well-known restaurant in Miami. Mark says it is essential to grill it slowly over a hardwood fire (in Jamaica it is cooked over allspice branches) for the right smoky flavor. We suggest using any available wood chips on the gas barbecue.

1 pork loin roast (2 to 2-1/2 lb.)

3 tbsp. whole allspice (or 2 tbsp. ground)

1/2 whole nutmeg or 2 tsp. ground

1 cinnamon stick or 1 tsp. ground

1 cup chopped Spanish onion

1 cup chopped green onion

3 tbsp. minced fresh ginger

1 scotch bonnet pepper (or other small, hot pepper), seeded and chopped

1/2 cup fresh orange juice

1/4 cup freshly squeezed lime juice

1/2 cup soy sauce

1/2 cup olive oil

Salt and freshly ground pepper

If using whole spices, toast allspice, nutmeg and cinnamon in a warm skillet. Grind in a spice mill. Combine all ingredients except pork in a food processor and blend until a thick paste is formed. Rub paste over pork loins and marinate, refrigerated, for 6 hours or more before grilling. Grill over very low heat on the barbecue until just cooked through, about 1 hour. Serve with black beans, corn, fried plantain and steamed yucca or rice.

Serves 4.

Jerk: According to Deura Dedeaux, author of The Sugar Reef Caribbean Cookbook, jerk refers to a method of cooking created by the Arawak Indians. The Indians poked, or "jerked," the carcass of an animal with holes and stuffed them with spices. The animal was placed in a deep pit with stones and green wood, and then smoked for hours.

GLAZED PORK LOIN

A glory that is Greek.

4 lb. boned pork loin

Orange-Spice Rub (*recipe follows*)

Fruit Stuffing (*recipe follows*)

1/2 cup red-currant jelly, warmed with 1 tbsp. lemon juice

Cut loin down center, but not all the way through; lay flat. Slit horizontally down each side. Rub half Orange-Spice into slits. Place stuffing in center; tie loin securely and rub remaining Orange-Spice Rub over exterior. Roast at 350°F for 15 minutes; pour over jelly. Continue to roast, basting with pan juices, about 1 1/2 hours, until a meat thermometer reads 160°F. Let stand 10 minutes before slicing.
Serves 6.

Orange-Spice Rub

2 tbsp. grated orange rind

1 tbsp. each salt and freshly ground pepper

2 tbsp. minced garlic

2 tbsp. each ground cumin and coriander

1/4 cup extra virgin olive oil

Combine ingredients well.

Fruit Stuffing

1 lb. lean ground pork

1/2 lb. pitted prunes, chopped

1/2 lb. kalmyrna dried figs, chopped

1 tbsp. grated orange rind

1 tbsp. minced garlic

1 tsp. each ground cumin and coriander

1 tsp. salt

Freshly ground pepper

Combine ingredients well.

SPARERIBS

NO MEAT IS SO SEMINAL TO THE AMERICAN SUMMER AS spareribs. Even if you eat them, Chinese and delivered, in the confines of an attic with nothing outside but the bleak bald-headed north, spareribs spell sun, wide-open spaces, backyard barbecues, chuck-wagons, hands cupped round a tin can and the remembrance of friends around every wood fire past ever gentle on the mind. And that's only half of it. Since they're also the world-champion lip-drooling mess-fest, ribs manage to be both sacred and profane at the same time—the Smithsonian and Madonna rolled into one. Some trick.

They can be cooked to advantage almost any way. Broiled, roasted and barbecued top the list, but Oriental kitchens also steam, braise and deep-fry them to excellent effect. However you do them, be confident with the sauce, marinade or seasoning: this is no time for subtlety.

Most important of all, Do Not Hurry. Any pork should be well cooked; ribs should be cooked over moderate heat to release excess fat and absorb the flavors of whatever sauce you've saddled them with. Close in importance is the rider: Do Not Dawdle. There is that magic point when ribs will be juicily succulent on the inside, glisteningly glazed on the out; coast very far past that point and they will turn to blackened boot leather.

Often it is a sound idea to parboil ribs first, 10 to 20 minutes, in well-seasoned water. This removes much unwanted fat and reduces the grilling time. After simmering, drain the ribs and leave to marinate in the fridge, preferably overnight.

Basting: Your chance for subtlety. Many baste too early in the secondary cooking. No matter how primal the urge to do so, beat it back; baste later. Failure to do so results too often in charred ribs and bitter spices, subtle as money down the drain.

Barbecue sauces: The best are always your own but how often do we make even remotely the same one twice in a row? Basic rule is add and taste, then taste and add. A sweet tooth? An extra spoonful of honey or brown sugar. Tarter? A touch more vinegar or lemon juice. Zestier? Another hit of Tabasco or Worcestershire, a couple pinches more of powdered mustard. Fancier? Add red wine and a mess of fresh herbs. Make more than you think you'll need and warm before using. The surplus will go excellently with chicken and the more robust fish.

BARBECUED RIBS

2 racks back spareribs (2 1/2 lb.)
3 tbsp. vegetable oil
1 small onion, sliced
1 lemon, sliced
1/2 cup water, wine, beer or stock
Barbecue Sauce (*recipe follows*)

Cut ribs into serving pieces. In a large skillet, brown well in oil. Toss in onion and lemon. Pour in wine. Partially cover. Reduce heat to a mere bubble. Go away and read a book. Forget about them. An hour or so later, they will be cooked; they should be very tender. Remove from liquid. You can now barbecue or broil them. Do this for 5 to 10 minutes, then baste with Barbecue Sauce or any other sauce that strikes your fancy.

Barbecue Sauce

2 tbsp. olive oil

1 small onion, chopped

1 cup tomato ketchup

1/2 cup water

2 tbsp. cider vinegar

2 tsp. dry mustard

3-inch piece orange rind

1/4 cup brown sugar

1 tbsp. lemon juice

2 tsp. Worcestershire sauce

In a medium saucepan over medium heat, soften onion in oil.
Add remaining ingredients and simmer 10 minutes. Cool. Keeps
refrigerated 1 week.
Makes 2 cups.

BBQ

THERE'S NO DOUBT THAT BARBECUING HAS MADE SOME advances from the days when the Carib Indians grilled their enemies on a grating of thin green sticks over an open fire. The Spanish called this operation the *barbacoa*—and with some horror, since they were sometimes the ones to end up on the thin green sticks.

That was centuries ago and we've all moved on a bit since then. A lot of the movement has been sideways, some of it backward, but in the matter of barbecues who can deny that our development has been all to the good? We're not using thin green sticks anymore.

Increasingly, North Americans use gas: in Canada about 80 percent of new barbecue sales go to propane, 15 percent (and rising) to natural gas (more expensive to buy, much less so to use, and inexhaustible, since the BBQ hooks into the house supply), 5 percent to charcoal; in the U.S. the gas–charcoal ratio is closer to 50-50, but the gas proportion is increasing sharply.

Easy to see why. Gas is cheap, there's no waste and the heat is as easy to regulate as the kitchen stove. *Cheap:* a barbecued meal that would cost no more than a dime to cook on propane uses up close to a dollar in charcoal. *No waste:* How much of that 10-lb. bag of charcoal wastes its sweetness on the desert air? It's a question fully understood by Colman's, makers of hot British powdered mustard, who admitted years ago that its profits were made from the mustard people left on their plates. The waste problem doesn't exist with the gas barbecue's constantly reusable lava or ceramic rocks. *Easy heat:* For the occasional BBQ griller, maddened by charcoal's lazy heat-gestation process and the subsequent hit-and-miss of raising or lowering the grill over the coals, this is gas's clearest, most undeniable advantage. Gas barbecues are the personal computers of the porch: once you use them you never go back.

Vegetables
Contrary to wide misconception, vegetables may be cooked on the barbecue to superb effect. Some are simply basted with flavored oil and grilled directly over medium-hot coals; others are best steamed in a protective foil pouch. Parboiling in some cases reduces grilling time and makes for more uniform cooking.

Unless you absolutely have to. Charcoal will always have its place as a backup (portability, picnics, and we're out of propane again) and as the common-sense choice for anyone who may barbecue no more than two or three times a summer. Then gas's cost advantage fades fast, since it doesn't factor in the cost of the equipment itself. This will run wherever your fancy takes you, from about $99 up to the middle hundreds for machines that could take you round the block for a trial spin. Even $99 would buy enough 10-lb. bags of charcoal to last the occasional user until well into the next millennium.

Still, at the end of the day, gas will always have Convenience and Lack of Mess on its side. For many, these are pearls way beyond price. Lastly, there's the matter of flavor: the matchless taste people think they get specifically from charcoal, they don't. Barbecuing is a generally healthy way to cook (it removes fat, most of it being drained off during the grilling) but the "charcoal" hit comes from the fat that hits the coals, flares up and sends back smoke and reworked aromas up from whence it came. Since the same thing happens when we cook over molten lava or ceramic briquets, a gas BBQ provides no loss of taste—unless you have a restless hunger for the subtleties that only charcoal starter fluid can impart to the simplest hamburger.

Safe as houses, gas. And then one remembers the annual horror story, with graphic closeups of smoking rubble, about a whole city block somewhere reduced to its component parts by a gas leak and an unwary match. Not a story often told around backyard barbecues.

And then there's this fellow falling through the sky at a terrible speed, unable to open his parachute. On his precipitous route earthward he sees someone coming upward at the same pace.

As they pass he yells: "Hey, know anything about parachutes?" " 'Fraid not," the other replies, hurtling into the ozone. "Know anything about gas barbecues?"

Barbecued Sausages and Peppers

Fine fare for the fall.

6 sausages (hot, spicy)

6 sweet peppers (red, green, yellow, with one hot if desired)

1 tbsp. olive oil

2 cloves garlic, finely minced

Salt and freshly ground pepper

Hot pepper flakes (optional)

6 long crusty rolls, heated

1 cup Basic Tomato Sauce (*recipe follows*)

Grilled Garlic

Allow 2 to 4 cloves of garlic per person. Rub each with olive oil and sprinkle with salt and pepper. Wrap in foil, and occasionally turn over medium coals at edge of grill about 1 hour.

Prick sausages and simmer in water until just cooked through, about 10 minutes. Grill whole peppers over coals until skins char and blister; immediately place in a bag. When cool, remove skins and seeds; slice. Set sausages over medium coals. Turn diligently until evenly browned about 10 minutes. (To have more crispy brown parts, split sausages after 5 minutes and brown cut surfaces.) Heat oil in a skillet over low heat. Add garlic, peppers, salt, pepper and pepper flakes; cook gently 10 minutes. Tuck each sausage into a hot roll, slather with tomato sauce and pile on cooked pepper mixture.
Serves 6.

Basic Tomato Sauce

2 tbsp. olive oil

1 onion, finely chopped (1/2 cup)

1 clove garlic, minced

1 can (28 oz.) plum tomatoes

1 can (5 1/2 oz.) tomato paste

1 tsp. dried basil

1 bay leaf

1/2 tsp. sugar

Salt and freshly ground pepper

*Heat oil in a large, heavy saucepan over medium-high heat. Add
onion and garlic; cook until softened. Stir in remaining ingredients,
mashing tomatoes with a potato masher to make a sauce-like
consistency, and simmer 30 minutes. Discard bay leaf.*
Makes 2 cups.

PEPPER STEAK

A grilled indulgence.

4 strip loin steaks, 1/2-inch thick

2 tbsp. coarsely ground black pepper

2 tbsp. butter

3 shallots, finely chopped

1 tsp. dried tarragon or 1 tbsp. fresh tarragon, chopped

1/4 cup port

1 cup demi-glace (*recipe follows*)

1/4 cup 35% cream

2 tbsp. green peppercorns, preserved in brine, drained

Sauté of Wild Mushrooms (*recipe on p. 57*)

*Rub steaks with pepper. Grill until cooked through, turning once,
about 8 to 10 minutes per side (rare or medium rare). Meanwhile,
melt butter in large skillet and cook shallots with tarragon until
softened. Stir in port; reduce by half. Swirl in demi-glace, heating
through. Stir in cream; reduce until lightly thickened. Add green
peppercorns. Spoon sauce over steaks, and top with mushrooms.
Serves 4.*

Demi-glace

This does not have the finesse of a classical demi-glace but will do the trick. Make brown stock in the usual way. Cook down briskly until reduced to 1 cup. It's easier to do this if you decrease the size of your pot as the broth reduces. Adjust seasoning. Better yet, find a store that stocks it.

Grilled Corn

Pull back husk carefully; remove the silk, not the leaves. Wrap the leaves up again, tie at the end and soak in water for 10 to 15 minutes. Barbecue 10 to 15 minutes (experiment here; time depends on your BBQ).

Husked corn may be grilled as well: cut in half and skewer. Cook until tender, brushing with melted butter, lemon juice and fresh herbs.

GRILLED LAMB WITH MINT SALAD

Lemon Vinaigrette (*recipe p. 67*)
1 lb. boneless lamb loin
1 bunch fresh spinach, washed and trimmed
Walnut Vinaigrette (*recipe follows*)
1/4 medium red onion, thinly sliced
1/2 cup crumbled feta
2 tbsp. chopped parsley
1 tbsp. fresh snipped mint
Salt and freshly ground pepper

Marinate lamb, covered, in Lemon Vinaigrette for several hours at room temperature or overnight in refrigerator. Remove, pat dry and barbecue or broil 3 to 4 minutes on each side; slice thinly. Toss spinach in some Walnut Vinaigrette, arrange on a large platter and garnish with lamb, onion, feta, parsley and mint; lightly season with salt and pepper. Drizzle over remaining vinaigrette.
Serves 4.

Walnut Vinaigrette

1 clove garlic, minced

1/4 tsp. salt

1 tsp. Dijon mustard

2 tbsp. red wine vinegar

6 tbsp. walnut oil (or part walnut, part safflower oil)

Freshly ground pepper to taste

Blend garlic with salt, mustard and vinegar. Whisk in oil. Season with pepper.

*A*SIAN SPICED LAMB

A year-round dish for the barbie.

1/4 cup Japanese soy sauce

2 tbsp. hoisin sauce

Rind of 1 orange, cut in strips

Juice of 1 orange

4 tbsp. lime juice

6 slices fresh ginger, peeled

4 cloves garlic, sliced

2 shallots, minced

1 tsp. sesame oil

1 tsp. red chili paste

1 tsp. five-spice powder, or ground cinnamon

1 boneless leg of lamb (about 3 1/2 lb.)

Combine marinade ingredients; mix well. Coat lamb with marinade. Marinate, refrigerated, overnight. Place in a roasting pan lined with foil (to help clean up). Roast at 325°F for about 1 hour, turning once; or barbecue, off direct heat, for about 1 hour, turning several times. Let stand 15 minutes before carving. Serve with steamed couscous. Serves 6.

Tip: This marinade is excellent for pork loins, flank or sirloin steak and chicken.

CURRIES AND STEWS

O F ALL FOREIGN DISHES, CURRY IS SURELY THE ONE THAT carries the largest freight to the imagination. The taste: musky, pungent, reeking of the East, mystery division. The country of origin: the India of the Taj Mahal. The uses: legion.

Pasta also means much to us, of course; but pasta *tutta sola* is unthinkable. Other foods must be imposed on pasta to ease it past the epiglottal stop; curry—no matter what the proportions of the ingredients—imposes itself indelibly on other foods. It is the ultimate despot of the kitchen, the more powerful for being benign.

Yet in many areas curry has not enjoyed a good press for years. Before widespread refrigeration, one of the uses of curry blends in hot climates was to conceal the taste of meats that were (more or less) going off. Decades later the ripple effect provokes sidelong looks at curries listed on restaurant menus—when they're there. And especially when they're there on Mondays.

Writers on Indian cooking—Indian writers above all— have been particularly fierce witnesses for the prosecution against curry-powder curries. Madhur Jaffrey may be the fiercest of the lot.

"The word 'curry,' " she instructs crisply in *An Invitation to Indian Cooking*, "is as degrading to India's great cuisine as the term 'chop suey' was to China's. No Indian ever uses curry powder in his cooking. It would make all dishes taste alike."

And so they would, if it were just a matter of proprietary-brand curry powders. But the tastes of curries are infinitely varied, depending on spices used, their freshness, the proportions of each when ground at home (no great hardship, as we shall see) and the culinary tradition followed.

The range of Indian cooking is daunting, and stretches back 4,000 years to the remarkable Indus civilization (advanced culture; bathing systems; enclosed, brick-lined sewers). When Mohenjo-Daro was excavated in 1921, in what is now Pakistan, the ancients were found to have invented the mortar and pestle, the food processor of its time, to grind the spices for the first curries. They were the world's first sophisticated seasoners of food—and their curries contained many of the same ingredients we find in use today.

Some confusion hums in the background about the origin of the word itself. *Kari* is (a) a Tamil (south Indian) word for sauce, (b) the name for a south Indian cooking technique and (c) the name of a small, aromatic tree native to Hindustan, in the north, but whose leaves are often used for *kari* dishes in the south. Other spices used for southern *karis* will likely include coriander, black pepper, cumin, fenugreek, cinnamon, mustard seeds and cloves; and the blend will be known as *kari podi* (or curry powder).

In the fullness of time, *kari* derivatives have spread throughout the world—not just to North America, where nine times out of ten we use the packaged stuff, but via countless regional variants in Sri Lanka, Myanmar (Burma), Thailand, Malaysia, Indonesia, Africa, the Netherlands and France. And notably in Trinidad, Jamaica and Guyana, where curries were introduced by indentured Indian workers who came over by the thousands in the mid-nineteenth century after the abolition of slavery.

Indians' methods with *kari* vary according to their many taboos and the local imperatives of agriculture. So vast a country can have no single cuisine; its regional cooking styles could occupy a lifetime's study.

If there's one loose linking factor in Indian foods, the umbrella they all share is spices—in all their variegated uses and endlessly changeable proportions. This mutability is the

---

Curry-Eating Specialist Fined

A stranger in an Indian restaurant in Southend [England] tried to demonstrate to Mr. Arthur Flint how he should eat his curried chicken and rice. Mr. Flint demonstrated his displeasure by pushing his curry in the stranger's face. In return, Mr. Flint received a blow on the head with a chair.

—Evening Standard, London, 1967.

key. What other common thread could stitch a country of Hindus and Sikhs (who won't eat beef); Hindu Brahmins (who won't eat onions and garlic either); Muslims and Jews (who won't eat pork); hardcore Hindu vegetarians (who won't eat tomatoes, red beets or watermelons, because of their red flesh); Bengali Hindu Brahmins (who, though largely vegetarian, do allow themselves fish and shellfish by adroitly arguing that these are vegetables of the sea); and the largely Christianized Goans, who will choke down anything?

Time for some links of our own.

CHICKEN IN RED CURRY PASTE

1 tbsp. oil

1 tbsp. red curry paste

1 and 1/3 cup coconut milk

2 stalks lemongrass, white part only, chopped

1 lb. boneless, skinless chicken, cut in strips

2 cups slivered bamboo shoots

1 tbsp. fish sauce

4 kaffir lime leaves

1 small hot green chili, seeded and sliced (optional)

1 tbsp. chopped coriander

Fresh lime juice

In a skillet over medium heat, heat oil with curry paste and coconut milk. Add lemongrass and chicken strips; simmer 10 minutes or until chicken is tender. Stir in bamboo shoots, fish sauce, lime leaves and chili (if using); heat through. Garnish with fresh coriander and a squeeze of lime juice.
Serves 4.

CURRIED CARIBBEAN CHICKEN

When you buy prepared curry powder, buy the best: check the ingredients' list and look for a wide variety of pure spices.

1 tbsp. curry powder (Caribbean style)

1 tbsp. paprika

1 tbsp. Worcestershire sauce

2 tbsp. lemon juice

6 tbsp. olive oil

1/4 tsp. hot sauce (Tabasco or other)

6 pieces chicken

2 onions, sliced

1/4 cup brown sugar

1 can (14-oz.) tomatoes, drained

Combine curry, paprika, Worcestershire sauce, lemon juice, 2 tbsp. oil and hot sauce. Marinate chicken pieces overnight. Sauté onions with brown sugar in remaining oil until onion is softened. Be careful not to burn sugar. Add chicken pieces and brown lightly on both sides. Add tomatoes and reserved marinade. Cover and cook until tender, about 40 minutes. To thicken, transfer chicken to dish in warm oven. Blend 1 tbsp. flour with 1/2 cup sauce until smooth. Return to pan, bring to boil and stir until nicely thickened. Serve with steamed yucca, fried plantain and light fluffy rice, or try with a whole lot of condiments: mango chutney, chopped apple and banana tossed with lemon or lime juice, peanuts, raisins, mandarin orange slices, papadums and shrimp chips.
Serves 6.

CURRIED LAMB LOIN WITH MANGO SALSA

1/2 cup yogurt
1 clove garlic, minced
1 tsp. coriander
1 tsp. cumin seeds crushed
1 tsp. garam masala
1 tsp. turmeric
1/2 tsp. ground nutmeg
1/2 tsp. ground cinnamon
1 tsp. paprika
1 small onion, minced
1 tsp. grated fresh ginger
4 lamb loins (2 lb., trimmed of fat) or boneless leg of lamb

*Combine all ingredients except lamb to make a marinade. Dry meat
well. Coat lamb well with marinade and let stand refrigerated,
overnight. Wipe off marinade. Barbecue or broil 3 to 4 minutes per
side until just rare. Boneless leg of lamb: sear on the barbecue then
cooked over indirect heat 1 to 1 1/2 hours. Slice thinly and serve with
Mango Salsa (recipe follows).*
Serves 4.

Mango Salsa
2 mangoes, peeled and finely chopped
1 small onion, finely chopped
1 clove garlic, minced
1 tbsp. finely chopped coriander
1 jalapeño, seeded and finely chopped
1 tbsp. freshly squeezed lemon juice
Salt and pepper

Combine all ingredients well. Let stand 1 hour to allow flavors to meld.
Makes 4 cups.

Tip: To peel mangoes: Turn sideways on end and cut straight down
against the flat side of the large center seed. Repeat on other side; then
trim both ends. Carefully cut away hard outer peel and slice.

STEWS

LAMB BOURGUIGNONNE

Rich and hearty fare; deeply restorative comfort food.

3 tbsp. butter

2 tbsp. vegetable oil

1 boneless leg of lamb (3 1/2 lb.)

1/2 cup all-purpose flour

1 tbsp. paprika

1/2 tsp. freshly ground pepper

4 cloves garlic, unpeeled

1 small onion, finely chopped

1 stalk celery, chopped

4 slices bacon, chopped

1 can (14 oz.) plum tomatoes

1/2 tsp. dried thyme

1 bay leaf

1 cup dry red wine

2 cups beef stock

4 carrots, peeled and sliced

1 cup pearl onions, peeled and blanched

1/2 lb. assorted wild mushrooms (shiitake, oyster, chanterelles)

2 tbsp. finely chopped parsley

Trim fat from lamb and cut meat in 3/4-inch cubes. Dry well. Combine flour, paprika and pepper. Toss with lamb. Shake off excess. In a large heavy pot over medium-high heat, heat 1 tbsp. butter and oil. Fry lamb until golden brown, adding a little extra oil if necessary. Transfer to a bowl and set aside. Add garlic, onions, celery and bacon to pan; sauté until lightly browned. Drain off fat. Return lamb to pot, add tomatoes, thyme, bay leaf, red wine and beef stock. Bring just to a boil. Lower heat and simmer partially covered, 1 hour or until meat is tender. In a skillet, toss and cook carrots and onions in 1 tbsp. butter

about 5 minutes. Add to stew. Continue simmering until just cooked through, about 20 minutes. Toss and cook mushrooms in remaining butter until lightly browned; stir into stew. Remove garlic cloves and squeeze out paste; blend well into stew. Discard bay leaf. Scatter with parsley.
Serves 8.

Variation: Use 2 lbs. of stewing beef instead of lamb. You may also substitute button mushrooms for wild.

Tip: To blanch pearl onions, dip in boiling water for 5 minutes. Rinse under cold running water. Snip off ends and peel.

BRAISED VEAL SHANKS

A hearty, herb-rich summer stew.

4 meaty veal shanks, preferably cut from the hindquarter
Salt and freshly ground pepper
Flour
2 tbsp. oil
4 tbsp. butter
2 tbsp. each finely minced celery, leek, carrots and onions
1 fresh tomato, diced
1 tbsp. minced parsley
4 cloves garlic, minced
1 tbsp. tomato paste
1 cup dry red wine
1/4 cup Madeira
1/2 tsp. each dried thyme and marjoram (or tsp. each fresh)
1/4 tsp. rosemary
1 bay leaf
1 cup (approx.) veal or chicken stock

Wipe veal shanks dry and season with salt and pepper; dip in flour and shake off excess. Heat oil in a heavy skillet and brown veal on all sides. Set aside. In a deep, heavy saucepan, heat 2 tbsp. butter, toss in minced vegetables, tomato, parsley and garlic; sauté briefly. Add tomato paste, veal and a sprinkling of flour. Continue to sauté until meat and vegetables become gloriously brown; be careful not to burn the flour. Stir in red wine, Madeira and herbs; allow to bubble for 1 minute. Pour in just enough stock to cover the shanks, bring to a boil, then lower the heat, cover and simmer until meat is tender. (Provimi veal take about 50 minutes. Darker veal will take about 15 minutes longer.) Discard bay leaf; adjust seasonings. (The dish may be prepared ahead to this point, stored in the refrigerator and gently reheated.) At serving time, heat remaining 2 tbsp. butter in a small skillet, swirling the pan as the butter turns nut brown. Glaze the veal shanks with browned butter. And give thanks to the Fatted Calf in all its forms. Serves 4.

Fish and Shellfish

P EOPLE HAVE BEEN CATCHING FISH FOR MORE THAN 100,000 years, the same time it has taken us to realize that at our current rate of greed they won't last forever. Already Newfoundland, whose history has been writ in fish for three centuries, has been brought to her knees by international—and her own—overfishing of the cod stocks of the great Grand Banks spawning ground (discovered, accidentally, around the year 1000 by Basque fishermen looking for whales). A far cry from the days when European explorers went home with goggle-eyed reports of New World seas and estuaries so thick with fish that boats had trouble getting through them.

Napoleon on the old religious custom of fish Fridays and fish Lent: "What idiots we are to believe that abstaining from flesh, and eating fish—which is so much more delicate and delicious— constitutes fasting!"

A far cry, too, from the days of Homer, who wrote, astonishingly, that fish was "wretched food, the last resource of shipwrecked sailors." Today we know what a remarkable resource they are for us all; rich in the fatty acids that fight the bad cholesterol and retard the development of heart disease—also in phosphorus, good for the brain. All we have to do, we descendants of sea creatures ourselves, is to use it with more intelligence. And remember where we came from.

There are some 20,000 species of fish around the world, of which we eat about 40. No reason not to broaden our sights a bit: inventive experimentation, with an encouraging hit or two of phosphorus, would do us no end of good.

Meanwhile, on with some fish that are not endangered. Yet.

Whole Fish With Garlic Sauces

For oven or barbecue, a feast either hot or cold. (Pictured opposite page 120.)

1 tbsp. olive oil

1 fish (3 to 4 lb.), gutted and cleaned (salmon, lake trout)

Salt and freshly ground pepper

1 small onion, sliced

2 sprigs parsley

1 bay leaf

1/4 tsp. fennel seeds

1/4 cup dry white wine

Garnishes: cherry tomatoes, tiny cooked green beans, sliced hard-cooked eggs, black olives, lemon slices

Lightly oil a large sheet of heavy foil. Place fish in center. Season cavity with salt and pepper. Tuck onion slices, parsley, bay leaf and fennel in cavity. Drizzle fish with a little more oil; pour over wine and season again. Wrap securely in foil. Place on grill over hot coals, or bake at 450°F. Allow about 10 minutes for each inch of the fish's thickness, plus 5 minutes for heat to penetrate foil. After 25 to 30 minutes, open package to test whether fish is cooked. (Fish should flake easily.) Transfer fish to a large platter. Carefully lift off top layer of skin and remove dark fat on flesh surface. Garnish. Accompany with the following classic garlic sauces: skordalia, rouille and aïoli. Serves 4 to 6.

Skordalia (*Walnut Garlic Sauce*)
A fine dip, too, for prepared vegetables. Use whole fresh nuts; skin, roast and grind them yourself.
1/2 cup fresh white breadcrumbs
2 to 4 cloves garlic
1/2 tsp. sea salt
1 cup finely ground walnuts
3/4 to 1 cup fruity olive oil
Juice 1 lemon, strained
Ripe olives

Soak breadcrumbs in cold water 5 minutes; squeeze until very dry. Pound garlic and salt in mortar with pestle or mix using a food processor; pound again with nuts and breadcrumbs to a smooth paste. Incorporate oil, a few drops at a time, until thick, then a few table-spoons lemon juice. Adjust flavor with oil, lemon or salt. Refrigerate, covered. Mound, and circle with olives.
Makes 2 cups.

Tip: This is excellent served on crostini as an appetizer.

Rouille
A fiery condiment served with grilled fish or stirred into fish soups.
1 slice French bread, crust removed
1/4 cup fish stock
3 to 6 cloves garlic
1/2 tsp. salt
1/4 cup puréed roasted red peppers
1/2 tsp. cayenne or a few drops hot pepper sauce
Freshly ground pepper
Pinch saffron
1/4 to 1/2 cup light olive oil

Soak bread in stock. Using a mortar and pestle, pound garlic with salt to make a purée. Stir in pepper purée and softened bread; season with cayenne, pepper and saffron. Whisk in enough olive oil to make a smooth sauce.
Makes about 1 cup.

Aïoli

A rich, pungent garlic mayonnaise, "the butter of Provence". Serve lavishly over mixed warm vegetables, with fish, egg dishes or lobster. Float a dollop in such robust fish stews as bourride or bouillabaisse. As Frédéric Mistral, Provençal poet, once put it: "It concentrates all the sun-loving gaiety of Provence in its essence, but it also has a particular virtue: it keeps flies away." As ever when making mayonnaise, have all ingredients at room temperature.

3 to 4 cloves garlic

1/2 tsp. salt

2 egg yolks

1 tsp. Dijon mustard

1 1/2 cups light olive oil, or half olive oil, half corn oil

2 tbsp. hot water

Freshly ground pepper

Lemon juice

Using a mortar and pestle, pound garlic and salt together to a paste; stir in yolks and mustard. Slowly whisk in oil, at first by drops and then in a steady stream. Beat in hot water to stabilize and lighten sauce. Adjust flavor with salt, pepper and lemon juice. Refrigerate. Allow to come to room temperature before stirring, or mayonnaise may break down.
Makes about 2 cups.

FISH À LA VERACRUZANA

Fish in a heavy olive and caper sauce from Mexico.

**1 firm-fleshed whole fish, such as red snapper or striped bass
(3 to 4 lb.)**

Juice of 2 limes, rinds reserved

Salt and freshly ground pepper

1/4 cup olive oil

1 cup chopped onions

2 cloves garlic, chopped

2 lb. tomatoes, peeled, seeded and chopped

1 bay leaf

1/2 tsp. dried oregano

12 stuffed green olives, halved

2 tbsp. capers, drained

2 jalapeños, finely chopped, more if you can stand it

Lime wedges and coriander sprigs for garnish

*Clean the fish but leave the head on. Prick the skin all over with a
fork and sprinkle with lime juice. Stuff lime rinds in the cavity.
Marinate several hours, refrigerated; remove the lime rinds. Season
fish with salt and pepper; lay it in a baking dish. Heat oil in a skillet.
Add onions and garlic; cook until soft. Add tomatoes, bay leaf,
oregano, olives, capers and jalapeños. Simmer 10 minutes; adjust seasoning. Discard bay leaf. Pour sauce over the fish. Bake at 375°F for
about 15 minutes. Carefully turn the fish over, baste with the sauce
and continue baking for a further 15 minutes or until the fish flakes
easily when tested with a fork. Garnish with lime wedges and coriander sprigs. Accompany with fragrant rice.*
Serves 6.

Barbecued Red Snapper With Red Pepper Sauce

1 whole red snapper (3 to 4 lb.)

3 limes

2 tbsp. oil

1 clove garlic, chopped

Salt and freshly ground pepper

Coriander leaves

Red Pepper Sauce (*recipe follows*)

Clean fish, prick skin and place in a shallow dish. Sprinkle inside and out with juice of 2 limes, oil, garlic, salt and pepper; marinate a few hours. Drain fish, reserving marinade, and pat dry. Barbecue or grill about 5 minutes per side, or until flesh just flakes, basting occasionally with marinade. Garnish with slices of remaining lime and coriander, and accompany with Red Pepper Sauce (recipe follows).
Serve 4 to 6.

This sauce is excellent tossed with warm pasta or used to replace Classic Tomato Sauce in Veal Cannelloni (p.00).

Red Pepper Sauce

1 onion, chopped

2 cloves garlic, chopped

2 tbsp. olive oil

2 cups tomatoes, peeled, seeded and chopped

1 to 2 fresh hot chilies, seeded and chopped

1/2 tsp. dried oregano

Salt and freshly ground pepper

Pinch sugar

1 tbsp. lime juice

1 sweet red pepper, roasted, peeled and seeded

In a skillet, sweat onion and garlic in hot oil until soft. Add tomatoes, chilies, oregano, salt, pepper, sugar and lime juice; simmer about 2 minutes. Add red pepper; purée until smooth; sieve.
Makes 2 cups.

TUNA NIÇOISE

Fresh tuna, in place of the usual canned, offers a lighter taste to this classic.

1 lb. fresh tuna, cut in chunks

1 green onion, sliced

1-inch piece fresh ginger, peeled and sliced

1 tbsp. olive oil

2 sprigs parsley

1/2 cup dry white wine

1/2 lb. French green beans, trimmed

8 small waxy potatoes

1 jar (4 oz.) marinated artichoke hearts

1 tsp. snipped chives

Tarragon Mayonnaise (*recipe follows*)

1 head Boston lettuce

2 hard-cooked eggs, sliced

1/4 cup niçoise olives

1 tbsp. chopped fresh chervil or parsley

Salt and freshly ground pepper

Poach tuna with onion, ginger, oil and parsley in wine and water to cover until cooked through, about 5 minutes. Drain and cool. Blanch beans; cool. Cook, cool and slice potatoes. Drain artichokes; slice. Gently toss together tuna, beans, potatoes, artichokes and chives. Fold in mayonnaise. Serve on a bed of Boston lettuce. Arrange egg slices on top. Sprinkle with olives and chervil; season with salt and pepper. Serves 4.

Tarragon Mayonnaise

2 egg yolks

1 tbsp. lemon juice

1 tbsp. tarragon vinegar

1 tbsp. Dijon mustard

3/4 light olive oil

Salt and freshly ground pepper

Whisk yolks with lemon juice and vinegar. Beat in mustard. Whisk in oil gradually until thickened (will be the consistency of a thick dressing). Season.
Makes 1 cup.

SALMON

SOME LOOK ON SALMON AS THE HOLIDAY INN OF THE deeps, No Surprises, North America's answer to Portugal's sardine. They have no soul. A salmon is beautiful and brave, and its life cycle one of the great romantic mysteries in the larger scheme of things, if there is one. More such mysteries and fewer scientific certainties and the world would be a happier place.

There are two salmon strains, the Atlantic (*Salmo salar*) and the Pacific (*Oncorhynchus*, of which there are five North American species). Roderick Haig-Brown (1908–1976), the Canadian naturalist whose writings on salmon must be second nature to anyone taking the subject seriously, maintained that this greatest of all swimming fish once ranged freely between the two oceans, and became separated, some two million years ago, by the buildup of Arctic ice.

For the past 150 years *Salmo salar* has had the worst of it, since it has had to cope with the massive industrialization of Europe and the eastern American seaboard. In the early 1800s, before dams and diversions, overpopulation and pollution, it abounded from Norway to Portugal, Labrador to Connecticut. Indeed, there was so damn much of it that *S. salar* was worse than a cliché, it was junk fish, and workers strove mightily to have their salmon intake reduced. In Norway, servants fought to get it down, legally, to five salmon meals a week. Domestics in colonial America must have been better organized: early on they managed to force laws on the books limiting salmon rations to no more than once a week. Knowing now the value of salmon's LDL-fighting omega-3 acids, we should be saying *at least*, instead of no more than. But there's humanity for you, never knowing a good thing.

The Pacific's five *Oncorhynchus* cousins have had a better time of it. Thanks to what the industry calls "resource enhancement" and tougher anti-overfishing laws out there, the Pacific harvest has had a series of record years starting in 1980.

Here science redeems itself. No other eating fish in the mass is so carefully tracked as the Pacific salmon, its numbers, sizes and ages so lovingly recorded. No other fascinates to the same degree. Consider the life cycle.

Somewhere, often hundreds of miles up some West Coast river, a hen salmon lays (let's say) 3,000 eggs, fertilized by the milt of the cock. Exhausted by their efforts, both—without exception, in contrast to Atlantic salmon, which often live to spawn again—die.

Of the 3,000 eggs, maybe thirty will survive to fingerling size. Of these thirty, fighting flood, drought, pollution, geese, gulls, bears, even dragonflies, on their voyage to the sea, three or four luckies will survive. After a year or more gaining strength in the river, they set out on their separate journeys, which will last two to seven years, depending on species, and cover thousands of miles, often in huge loops (the sockeye averages about 2,000 miles annually). And then, biological clock ticking, they head home.

This is the part that blows the scientific mind, let alone a romantic one. From thousands of miles distant and from half the points of the compass, they arrive home—late June or, oh, early July, Mavis, if I stop in the Aleutians for a spot of R-'n'-R—within three weeks of one another. In a 10-year survey at Alaska's Bristol Bay, the sockeye timed their return with such accuracy that the return run never varied *more than eight days*. And when they return home it is not any old home, somewhere vaguely along their native coast. It is to *their* estuary, *their* river, the selfsame river where they were spawned.

How on earth do they find it? Many are the theories; hard answers are few. Their exquisite sense of smell, perhaps? (Salmon can detect dilutions of one part in a billion.) Navigation by the sun and stars? Electrical impulses detected from the earth's magnetic field? Presumably one day we'll know for sure, but not soon, pray God. Let it remain a glorious biological mystery for another eon or so.

However they manage it, it's plainly second nature to them now. But here the hard part begins. The salmon arrive back at the estuary in peak condition and hang about for a bit, fat and sassy (and catchable), ready to take on the world, boring one another puce with travel stories. And after a bit they head upstream—only now, for some other reason we can only guess at, they stop eating *entirely* and thus make an already fearful journey infinitely harder.

Once their stored up fat is exhausted, their stomachs shrivel, their unused jaws turn into grotesque hooks, they become little more than egg-and-sperm banks. They further weaken themselves by fighting the current for months on end and by constantly leaping up and over falls twice the height of tall men.

Through it all their spirit (instinct, if you prefer) remains undaunted: mile after mile, week after week, they will ignore that fork, bypass that tributary, until they have made their way, wasted and wounded, to the precise spawning grounds where they were born. There hen and cock lie side by side gathering what strength remains, until the female deposits her (let's say) 3,000 eggs.

Over to Haig-Brown, the sage of Campbell River, Vancouver Island, the Boswell of the salmon brooks, and the closing lines of *Return to the River* (1946), his moving but rigorously unsentimental story about the life of a salmon called Spring:

"Her tail moved once or twice, feebly, but all the urgencies, all the desires that had driven life through her were spent. So she lay quietly across the stream flow, drifting, as no strong salmon does; and the water opened her gill plates, and forced under them, and she died."

No other resource offers mankind so much in return for so little.
—*Roderick Haig-Brown.*

BARBECUED SALMON AND GREENS

This particular marinade is excellent for whole salmon sides, salmon trout and firm white fish.

1 tsp. sesame oil

1/2 cup Japanese soy sauce

1 tbsp. honey

2 tbsp. lemon juice

2 cloves garlic, peeled and halved

2 slices fresh ginger, peeled

2 green onions, sliced

2 lb. fresh salmon tail, boned, skin on or 4 salmon trout fillets, skin on

6 cups assorted greens (including arugula)

1 recipe Red Wine Vinaigrette (*recipe follows*)

Garnish: herbs, salmon caviar, slivered shiitake mushrooms sautéed in vegetable oil and seasoned with a touch of sesame oil and lemon juice

Freshly ground pepper

Whisk together sesame oil, soy sauce, honey, lemon juice. Add garlic, fresh ginger and green onions. Spoon over salmon and marinate, refrigerated, 1 hour. Place on a lightly oiled grill, skin side down. When edges turn pink and a spatula is easily slipped between flesh and skin (about 5 minutes), carefully lift and turn; leave 3 to 4 minutes. The salmon should be rare on the inside. Toss greens with vinaigrette. Divide between 4 plates. Slip a piece of warm salmon on top of the greens and scatter garnish and freshly ground pepper on top. Serves 4.

Red Wine Vinaigrette

2 tbsp. red wine vinegar

2 tbsp. olive oil and 1 tbsp. walnut oil
   (or 2 1/2 tbsp. olive oil and 1/2 tsp. sesame oil)

1 slice fresh ginger, grated

1 clove garlic, peeled, halved

1 tsp. minced shallot

Salt and freshly ground pepper to taste

Combine; let stand 30 minutes. Strain.

GRILLED SALMON AND GOAT CHEESE BAGUETTE

Conceived on the first warm sunny day, of a very long cold winter, at the foot of a ski hill in Ellicottville, NY—that Aspen of the East.

4 garlic cloves, peeled

4 tbsp. olive oil

1 lb. smoked salmon, sliced, skin on

1/2 cup soft goat cheese

1/2 thinly sliced sweet onion

2 roasted red/yellow peppers, seeded peeled and sliced

1 small bunch arugula

12 fresh basil leaves

Freshly ground pepper

A squeeze of lemon juice

Slice baguette diagonally into 3/4 inch slices (8 to 10 slices). Brush with olive oil. Set on grill. Brown lightly on both sides. Rub bread well with cut end of garlic clove. Brush skin of smoked salmon with olive oil and slide on barbecue just to warm. Spread goat cheese on grilled bread, top with salmon (skin removed), a grind or two of black pepper and a squeeze of lemon juice. Pile on pepper, or arugula and basil leaves. Serve with a good Spanish rioja.

Serves 4.

Tip: If salmon does not have skin, place sliced salmon on a piece of oiled tin foil, poked with several holes.

SOLE

THEY ARE WONDERS, FLATFISH; SITTING THERE FLATLY on the fishmonger's counter, they are easily taken for granted. Flat, round and they taste good is as much emotion as they can raise in most of us. Profile, no depth.

But consider the path they take to get there. What makes flatfish fascinating is that none of them starts out that way: as small fry, all begin as if they intended to develop into normal, fully rounded fish—salmon, say, or bass. But following the counsel of millennia of genetics, the infant flatfish soon reject this route and opt for the two-dimensional.

And so one eye moves from one side of the head to join its mate on the other: some (the brill, the turbot) prefer their eyes on the right, others (sole, plaice, flounder) prefer them on the left. As the fish flattens out, the eye-side now becoming the top, lookout side, the mouth is twisting in the opposite direction, the better to syphon up the organisms lying beneath it. All adapted by the ages for bumming around lazily in the depths, which gives flatfish their secondary name, bottom-feeders.

The fact that these changes occur early in their lives—the sole has modified itself by the time it's about an inch long—hardly diminishes the wonder that they occur at all. Or perhaps, since their destiny is to be bottom-feeding flatfish: why didn't they kick off that way at birth?

Sautéed Sole with Tomato Saffron Sauce

Sole is splendid unadulterated, with a squeeze of fresh lemon or served with a delicate sauce.

Classic Tomato Sauce, flavored with saffron (*recipe on p. 85*)

1 tbsp. capers, drained

6 sole fillets (2 1/2 lb.)

2 tbsp. unsalted butter

1 tbsp. finely chopped parsley

2 tbsp. grated Parmesan cheese

Heat tomato sauce in a saucepan. Stir in capers. Dry fish well. Gently cook in hot butter in a large, heavy skillet until just cooked through, turning once. Transfer to a warm platter. Spoon sauce over fillets; sprinkle with parsley and Parmesan cheese. Serve with a crusty baguette and a chilled white burgundy.
Serves 4.

Variation: Sole may be brushed with melted butter and cooked 4 inches from broiler until just cooked through.

Fritz Karl Watel (1635–1671), later Vatel, was a Franco-Swiss chef-administrator to the noble house of Chantilly. In 1671 he had the task of organizing a major celebration in honor of Louis XIV, the Sun King, and 3,000 of his closest friends. This extended *cochon hors*, or pig-out, was to be held over several days and included a hunting party and a fireworks display.

Not everything went according to plan: bad weather spoiled the fireworks, and some unexpected guests—one can only guess at how many, over and above the 3,000—caused meat shortages. A brittle sort, Vatel took these setbacks as a stain on his honor. The last straw came when he discovered, on the second day of the celebration, that not enough fresh fish had been delivered for that day's meals. Vatel snapped, a sound that echoes through the higher reaches of French cuisine to this day.

"I shall not survive this disgrace," he sighed, retired to his quarters and fell on his sword at the very moment that new wagonloads of fish were trundling through Chantilly's gates.

LOBSTER

A NASTY PIECE OF WORK, THE LOBSTER, UNTIL WE GET around to eating it. Behind its beady little eyes lies a nature at once timid and vicious. The pegs or sturdy rubber bands restraining its claws in the fishmonger's tank are less to protect us than its fellows: without them it would batten on one of its weaker brethren or sistren with a cannibalistic fury.

Still, ancient as it is—it has changed hardly at all in 10,000 years—and low though it may be on the evolutionary scale, the human race has for centuries been putting it to death in more sophisticated ways than the lobster has ever had at its disposal. Since we're at the top of the food chain we can assure ourselves nervously—just as we're about to thrust it, thrashing about in transports of what looks suspiciously like pain, deep into a few gallons of furiously boiling water—that of course the lobster doesn't actually *feel* very much, you know.

Not to be too anthropomorphic about it, the lobster's whistling squeal as it goes under for the last time is in fact an evacuation of wind; its final fart, so to speak. Doubtless early missionaries found themselves in much the same position when their conversion efforts in foreign seas went badly wrong.

The most popular lobster on this continent is *Homarus americanus,* from the eastern seaboard, though its clawless cousin the rock lobster (a.k.a. spiny lobster, langouste, cray- and crawfish) is a prime source of lobster tails. Rich in protein and mineral salts, low in fat (90 calories per 100 g), each is easy to prepare, as delicious cold as hot, as celebratory as champagne.

God surely moves in mysterious ways, for these dining paragons not only are relatives of *Blattella germanica* (the justly hideous scientific handle for the common cockroach) but also spend most of their lives eating decaying fish, the more rotten the better. Thus the fisherman's rule of thumb when setting bait: "Fresh for crab, rank for lobster." As a 2-lb. lobster lands in front of us in all its glory after some dozen years scavenging around the filth it finds in estuaries and on the ocean floor, we can only wonder at the end result: a kind of purgative in reverse.

But God knows we move in mysterious ways, too. A hundred years ago lobsters could barely be given away. In 1886 the going price on the northeastern seaboard was 2 cents per pound. Old-timers still remember when the great crustaceans were so little regarded that they used to pick them up at low tide, tangled in seaweed, and mash them for chicken feed.

Sesame-Dressed Lobster Salad

4 live lobsters (each 1 1/4 to 1 1/2 lb.)

Basic Fish Fumet (*p. 26*)

Sesame Dressing (*recipe follows*)

Mixed salad greens, washed and dried

1 each sweet red and yellow peppers, roasted, skinned and chunked

Snipped fresh herbs

Slivered lemon rind

2 tbsp. toasted sesame seeds

Cook lobsters in simmering Fish Fumet and water, 7 to 10 minutes. Remove tail meat in one piece and slice into medallions; leave claw meat whole for garnish. Chunk remaining meat, toss in a little sesame dressing and arrange over greens and peppers on a platter. Overlap medallions on top. Drizzle with remaining dressing. Scatter with herbs, lemon rind and sesame seeds. Garnish with claws.
Serves 4.

Sesame Dressing

1 clove garlic

1 tsp. Dijon mustard

1 egg yolk

2 tbsp. sherry vinegar

2 tbsp. soy sauce

1 tbsp. sesame oil

1 1/2 cups safflower oil

Lemon juice

Freshly ground pepper

Briefly whirl garlic, mustard, egg yolk, vinegar and soy sauce in food processor. With motor running, slowly add oils. Blend in lemon juice and pepper. Cover and refrigerate.
Makes 1 1/2 cups.

SHRIMPS

FOR MANY PEOPLE SHRIMP SEEM TO OCCUPY THE SAME sort of position in the pantheon of taste as the best barbecued ribs. We remember shrimp orgies in the most moistly precise ways, as others remember assassinations; thus echoing the French, who when the earth moves for them call it "the little death."

Shrimp is a vague word. It stands for various members of the Decapoda order (crustaceans with 10 legs) and usually includes the larger prawns, but not crawfish or langouste, which are species of spiny lobster. Scampi is the trendy name of choice in restaurants, meaning they feel free to charge more for them; but genuine scampi, large Italian prawns from the Adriatic, rarely surface on this side of the Atlantic, and shrimp often substitute, unacknowledged, in Italy, too.

Most shrimp we buy here are white shrimp from the coasts of the Gulf of Mexico and the Caribbean. But thanks to refrigeration we also have ready access to brown shrimp (from the western side of the Atlantic), to pink shrimp (parts of the Atlantic), to the sidestripe (California to Alaska) and to the great tiger shrimp and the kuruman (Thailand and Japan).

What matters most to fishermen is size: the bigger the shrimp, the more they charge. They do this because the market supports them: shrimp eaters believe that bigger (say, 10-to-a-pound) taste better than smaller (70-and-up-to-a-pound). But freshness is what's best of all, at which point size no longer matters.

Rich in protein, minerals and vitamins, poverty-stricken in calories, shellfish have long enjoyed a reputation, among the susceptible, for aphrodisiac potency. The susceptible for some reason ignore the literature that says it's all baloney (itself as aphrodisiac as saltpeter), and in the case of

Shrimp sex: Ambiguous, experimental, easily bored, therefore madly chic. Most shrimp spend their first two years as males, princes of the tides, taking pleasure where they find it. Then, for reasons undivulged, they change sex and spend the rest of their lives as highly domestic females, rarely straying from home. One can but marvel.

shrimp would call as a witness King Lapetamaka II, whose exploits were recorded by a shipmate of the British explorer Capt. James Cook during his Pacific voyage of discovery in 1778.

Lapetamaka, in his eighties, explained chattily to the diarist that he regarded it as his royal obligation to deflower every maiden in his island kingdom; that he was still discharging his royal duties eight to ten times every day, and that shrimp, and plenty of them, were his secret to the successful exercise of the divine right of kings. Thus encouraged, read on.

The second most popular seafood in North America (after tuna), shrimp often get knocked for their cholesterol content. It is the one general caveat fish lovers have about them. True, shrimp contain more cholesterol than any other shellfish except squid: 150 mg per 3 1/2 oz. serving. But they're right at the low end in saturated fat (0.3 g), which raises blood cholesterol much more sharply than dietary cholesterol does.

Compared with beef, which is lower in cholesterol but higher in calories and packs up to 30 times the amount of saturated fat, shrimp are eminently good for us. Plus they boast something beef can never have: omega-3s, fish-oil's fatty acids that are good for the heart.

GAMBAS AL AJILLO

For the recluse only; even parsley and coriander won't help here.
The shell keeps the shrimp beautifully tender.

1 1/2 lb. large shrimp in their shells
1/4 cup butter
2 tbsp. olive oil
8 cloves garlic, halved
Salt to taste
Juice of 2 lemons (4 tbsp.)

Place shrimp under cold running water; dry well. Heat butter and olive oil in a heavy skillet over high heat. Toss in shrimp and garlic; sauté until shrimp are bright pink and tender. Sprinkle with salt and lemon juice. Serve immediately. To eat: Suck the juice from each shell, peel, dip the shrimp back in the sauce and enjoy. Cloth napkins are definitely in order, as is a well-chilled Fume Blanc and a Gulf of Mexico view.
Serves 4 good friends, barely.

GREEK SHRIMP

Classic Tomato Sauce (*recipe on p. 85*)
1/2 tsp. dried oregano
1/4 tsp. fennel seeds
1/2 cup white wine
1 1/2 lb. shrimp, washed, peeled, well dried
1/4 Bulgarian feta, crumbled
1 tbsp. finely chopped parsley
1 lemon

Prepare tomato sauce as described, adding oregano and fennel with bay leaf. Heat tomato sauce in a large skillet over moderate heat; add wine, and reduce slightly. Toss in shrimp; cook about 5 minutes. Stir in feta and parsley; heat through. Discard bay leaf. Flavor with a good squeeze of lemon. Serve with saffron rice.
Serves 4.

WARM SALAD OF SCALLOPS AND SHRIMP WITH GINGER DRESSING

The salad greens should be a pleasing mix of color, texture and flavor. Simplicity itself to prepare.

2 tbsp. clarified butter

8 scallops, sliced

1 tomato, peeled, seeded and chopped

2 dried (or fresh) shiitake mushrooms, soaked, drained and sliced

2 tbsp. julienned carrot

8 snow peas, blanched

8 large shrimp, peeled and cooked

2 tbsp. Ginger Dressing (*recipe follows*)

Colorful salad greens, such as radicchio, botavia, et al.

2 tsp. chopped coriander

Heat butter in skillet over medium heat. Toss in scallops; cook 5 to 10 seconds. Add tomato, mushrooms, carrot and snow peas; toss about 1 minute. Add shrimp. Pour off butter and stir in Ginger Dressing. Heat through. Arrange salad greens attractively on plates and spoon scallops on top. Sprinkle with coriander and serve at once.
Serves 1 as an entree, 2 as an appetizer.

Ginger Dressing

1 tsp. minced fresh ginger

1/3 cup Japanese rice vinegar

1 tbsp. soy sauce

1/2 tsp. brown sugar

1/4 tsp. hot chili paste or oil

1/4 cup sesame oil

3/4 cup sunflower oil

Steep ginger in vinegar overnight. Combine with remaining ingredients. Whisk well to blend. Keeps well in a covered jar. Makes 1 to 1 1/2 cups.

SQUID

SQUID IS NOT A LOVELY NAME NOR A LOVELY FISH, UNTIL you get it down on the plate. A better name would be "sea clerk," as the English used to call it, since it has both pen (its vestigial bone or shell) and ink (a fluid it shares with its relatives the octopus and the cuttlefish). On the plate, provided it is not overcooked, it is always a revelation to anyone who has seen it in the whole, and raw, and has then gone to the trouble of preparing it. Once in the mouth, all reservations vanish.

In all conscience, there is nothing spiritually rewarding about cleaning squid, and you may prefer to take the easy way out and have the fishmonger do it. On the other hand, there are always those, possessed of stern inner fiber, who relish the challenge and believe that psychic avoidance is only cowardice abetted by laziness. They are the people who tackle Mount Everest because it is there and remain forever undaunted by the crabgrass in the garden of life. Squid preparation is designed specifically with these very special people in mind:

• Seize the beast by the tail with one hand and grasp the head and tentacles with the other.

• Pull gently, preferably over a newspaper, and all the innards should evacuate at one fulfilling go. A small transparent cartilage running along the back should be removed as well.

• Peel away the reddish mottled skin and turn the body inside out, rinsing well under cold water.

• Pull off the fins. Set aside.

• Now the head. Ignoring the sightless little eyes facing upward, sever the tentacles from the head and pop out the small cartilage tucked away at the base of the tentacles.

• The fins, body and tentacles are now ready to cook. The rest may be discarded, but the ink is well worth saving and using as a highly nutritious flavoring agent for pasta or rice (with squid/cuttlefish/octopus/shrimp odds and ends) at another time.

   • This ink is carried in a small silvery black sac nestled in the entrails just behind the head. Cut out the sac with a sharp knife, then press contents through a sieve. It is a matter of moments, simplicity itself, and barely noticeable considering all that has gone before.

   Next stop, Everest.

CALAMARES FRITOS

Is anything more rewarding for a big snack attack?

1 lb. squid, cleaned and cut in rings

1/2 cup all-purpose flour

4 eggs, beaten

1 cup light olive oil for frying

Salt to taste

Lots of lemon juice

Dry squid well. Place flour in a plastic bag. Add squid; shake until well coated. Dip in beaten eggs. In a heavy skillet, fry a few at a time in hot oil (not smoking)—turning once—until tender, about 10 to 12 minutes. Sprinkle with salt and a good squeeze lemon juice. Serve very hot.

Serves 1 calamares addict or 4 normal souls.

Tip: These are good served with yogurt, flavored with finely chopped red onion, lots of chopped dill and sugar to taste.

Since olive oil does burn at high temperatures, it helps to use a very light oil or use 1/2 vegetable oil, 1/2 olive oil.

OYSTERS

THE ROMANS ARE CREDITED WITH LEARNING HOW TO cultivate oysters—Sergius Aurata was farming them in 102 BC—but we owe to the French the oyster's latter-day popularity. And the French came upon it by accident, when in 1868 a boatload of Portuguese oysters capsized in the Bay of Biscay. They quickly established themselves in the Gironde estuary—and were so diligently harvested that a few years later oyster-gathering was outlawed during the bivalve's summer breeding season.

Hence the superstition that oysters should be avoided in months without an *r* in them, for reasons of one's health. For this there has never been any basis in fact; even less now than then, with the wonders of refrigeration.

These days the oyster is carefully farmed, its junior years out at sea, then for its maturity in fattening beds at the mouth of seagoing rivers. Its intriguing sexuality remains unchanged in its changeability: starting life as a male, it becomes a female after a year, and later reverts every now and then to a male just to keep its hand in. Thus the oyster passes through life as both mother and father—sexual ambivalence in the service of economy—but isn't much good being either. It will lay and fertilize 20 to 100 billion eggs at a time: only a few will grow up since mom-and-dad makes no effort to look after them at all.

Perhaps it's just as well. There's something about the oyster that brings out the glutton in oyster lovers as it is: multiply their availability by 20 or 30 billion and who knows what else we'd find to do but shuck and eat, eat and shuck, until the long day is ended. Two cases as a warning to us all: Diamond Jim Brady (1856–1917), the New York trencherman who thought nothing of downing five dozen of them a day (as well as, *on the same day*, six to eight lobsters, half a dozen crabs, two ducks, a large steak, two pounds of chocolate and fresh orange juice by the gallon); and Vernon Bass, who on

November 23, 1975, got his name into the *Guinness Book of Records* by ingesting 588 oysters in 17 minutes and 32 seconds in Sarasota, Florida. Oysters help prevent goiter, are good for our teeth, keep our legs straight and skin pure, and are fine food for the brain; but surely this is going a bit far?

To open: Scrub the shells under cold running water. Then hold the oyster with the hinge away from you, flatter side up. Near the hinge, insert the tip of a sturdy knife and twist. Move the blade to and fro to sever the muscle. Pull away the top shell and the oyster lies there before you in all its living glory, and its juices. Slide the knife under the meat to release it from the base.

To serve fresh: Open the oysters just before you need them. Serve icy cold on a mound of crushed ice, with lemon wedges, a pepper mill and plenty of good brown buttered bread to hand. Pick up oyster on pointed fork, with shell under chin; guide into mouth, chew once, close eyes as it slurps down, quick as you can say Vern Bass, to its goiter-preventing, brain-enhancing destiny. Remember, as you chase it down with a grateful sip of cool Chablis or Champagne, that it took the ambivalent oyster at least three years to get there.

The ancient Greeks, having invented democracy, liked to vote, and in the early days voted undesirables into exile by writing their names onto oyster shells, or ostrakones. Aristides the Just, a general known for his implacable integrity, was an early victim, despite the probity. Came the exile-voting day when an illiterate citizen, not recognizing Aristides, asked if he would help him write a name down on his ostrakon. Helpful as well as just, Aristides said yes—what name? "Aristides," said the illiterate.

The general, who must have wondered where probity got you, asked as he signed his own name onto the ostracizing oyster if he had ever done the man any harm. "No," the peasant answered, "but I'm sick and tired of hearing him always called 'the Just.' "

OYSTERS POACHED IN CHAMPAGNE ON A BED OF LEEKS

Traditional flavors in a "new" polygamous marriage. Although it's hard to imagine any real improvement on a well-chilled oyster opened and consumed on the spot with a well-chilled Veuve Clicquot.

2 lb. leeks

1/2 cup unsalted butter

Salt and freshly ground pepper

16 fresh oysters in the shell

1 cup champagne (or white wine)

1 tbsp. minced shallot

1/4 cup 35% cream

2 tbsp. very cold unsalted butter

Don't waste time looking for pearls. In the oysters that come our way any pearls you may find will be dull, small, utterly valueless. The pearls that mean something occur in oysters bred in the tropics— and their meat is inedible. The gods work these matters out over brandy and cigars.

Trim leeks, reserving white part and about 1 inch of green; halve and wash thoroughly. Cut into thin 2-inch slivers. Melt 1/2 cup butter in a heavy saucepan over gentle heat. Add leeks; season lightly with salt and pepper. Cook covered, stirring occasionally, about 20 minutes, or until leeks are very soft. Set aside and keep warm. Remove oysters from shells and place, with their liquor, in a small saucepan. Add champagne, shallot and a pinch more salt and pepper. Set pan over moderate heat. When liquid is just about to boil, lift out oysters with slotted spoon; keep warm. Reduce poaching liquid to 3/4 cup. Stir in cream; reduce again to 1/2 cup. Remove from heat and whisk in remaining butter piece by piece. Adjust seasoning. Divide leeks among 4 small plates. Top each plate with four oysters, spooning over a little sauce.

Serves 4.

MUSSELS

THE MYSTERY ABOUT MUSSELS IS WHY IT TOOK THEM SO long to gain favor in North America. They abound on both sides of the Atlantic but until recently their piquant cousin the clam, similarly plentiful both there and here, was beating them, in this hemisphere, hands down and going away.

Why didn't European colonists bring their mussel-eating habits with them? For some reason the French in Quebec, Acadia and Louisiana, the English in New England, the Dutch in New Amsterdam embraced the clam instead. It's clam, not mussel, chowder.

The smoking gun of legend points to the Indians, who are said to have warned the new immigrants that American mussels were lethally poisonous. The immigrants believed them, and by the time reason prevailed the anti-mussel pattern on this side of the water was set.

So goes legend, but not very far. For one thing, not all Indians had a thing against mussels; and those who did tended not to eat shellfish at all. For another, where were the pollutants to make them so lethal? No pesticides, no oil spills—and no copper, one of the mussel's chief toxic sources today. And for a third, mussel middens have been found on the west coast that prove the Indians of the Pacific were enjoying them in great quantities since at least 3500 BC.

And why not? Certainly on the wrong day the mussel can be very bad news: if there are poisons around—particularly a species of plankton called dinoflagellate, every bit as painful as it sounds—it will pick them up, distill them and pass them vengefully on, 100 proof, causing us anything from diarrhea at one end to paralysis and occasional death at the other.

But what kind of foodie wimps have we become if we let such rare considerations blind us to living? We have only to take sensible precautions—such as avoiding mussels in high summer and heeding government warnings designed to take the precautions for us. The payoff is an astoundingly efficient and nutritious mollusk: plentiful, cheap, easy to digest and delicious into the bargain.

Consider the nutrient comparisons between the mussel, for instance, and beef. Weight for weight both offer the same amount of protein, but from there on it's all in the mussel's favor: 50 percent more iron, nearly twice as much phosphorus (good for the brain and the nervous system), eleven times more calcium; all for 75 percent fewer calories and 95 percent less fat. Among shellfish, none—not the clam, not even the oyster, the rich person's mussel—gives better food value. All this without calculating the monstrous additional costs in land, feed and transportation to get that T-bone onto the plate.

Given the choice, should we buy wild or cultured? Either is delicious, but the cultured tends to be plumper, safer (particularly if you prefer them raw, as in southern France) because it is grown under controlled conditions, and cleaner, requiring only a rinse before its ultimate dispatch.

The wild ones, since they've been dredged from the ocean floor, need a thorough soaking and rinsing. Many swear by them, citing taste benefits only the rude would question. A friend of ours, who buys only wild, actually feeds them.

"I give them a spoonful or so of cornmeal in their soaking water," she says. "They love it—they spit out the bad bits from all their recent dinners and gorge on the good stuff. Then they settle down for a nap which is when I leap into action. I like to think they've quietly passed away."

In fact, they've anything but. But at least the condemned had a hearty breakfast.

Whichever you choose, wild or cultured, the mussels should be eaten on the day they are bought. Make sure the mussels you buy are zippered tight. Give a small squeeze to any slightly and inquisitively open one: a live one will snap shut. Discard any that don't: these are not inquisitive but dead. Similarly discard any that are cracked, or weigh a ton (they've ingested too much sand).

Scrub well under running water, cutting off the black hairy threads on the side. Known as the byssus, these possess a strength you'd never guess when gazing on them for the first, or umpteenth, time. The mussel attaches its byssus to any support at hand, which is how they establish colonies. (In ancient Greece, fishermen used gloves woven of byssus threads, which were so strong they were handed down, manually if one may say so, from generation to generation. The only trick was to keep them wet at all times: without water the byssus decays at once, much like Samson without his hair.)

Then, soak one hour. Repeat rinsing if water looks sandy.

Steaming, the simple method of choice: Prepare a seasoned brew of your own devising (wine, beer, herbs, fish stock). Simmer the mussels, covered, in a large wide-mouthed pot until the shells open. Stir occasionally. Discard, with appropriate speed, any that don't open. If preparing five dozen or more, use a wide roasting pan and cook in the same broth, foil-covered, in a 350°F oven.

Beyond steaming, mussels can handle many flavors so long as you know when to stop. The essential: never overcook. This turns mussels into Michelins and wrecks the whole enterprise.

MUSSELS IN ORANGE SAFFRON SAUCE

Compulsive eating, but not dainty. Serve in huge wide bowls with lots of crusty bread and heaps of napkins. (Pictured opposite page 121.)

4 lb. mussels

2 oranges

2 finely chopped shallots

1/4 cup finely chopped onion

2 tbsp. butter

1 cup dry white wine

2 bay leaves

1 tbsp. finely chopped fresh tarragon

1 tbsp. finely chopped fresh thyme

1/2 cup 35% cream

1/4 tsp. saffron

Salt

Freshly ground pepper

Chives, snipped

Scrub mussels well under running water, scraping off beards; soak 2 to 3 hrs, changing water twice. Juice oranges after carefully removing and slicing peel into strips. In a large, heavy pot, briefly sauté shallots and onion in melted butter until nicely softened. Add wine, juice, orange peel, bay leaves, tarragon, thyme; simmer 5 minutes, then bring to a boil. Drain mussels discarding any that are open. Toss mussels into pot and cook briskly (but not boiling), covered, 5 to 10 minutes until tender and just opened—stirring occasionally. Ladle mussels into a large bowl; cover to keep warm. Reduce sauce slightly (about 1 minute), and swirl in cream and saffron; taste, and adjust seasoning. Spoon mussels into wide soup bowls, ladling on sauce and dusting with chives.

Serves 4.

MEDITERRANEAN SEAFOOD SALAD

Don't be bound by this selection of shellfish: use whatever is best at the market.

1 lb. shrimp in the shell, well rinsed

1/2 lb. sea scallops, well rinsed

2 tbsp. lemon juice

1 lemon, sliced

12 mussels, well scrubbed

12 clams, well scrubbed

1 roasted sweet red pepper, skinned and cut in strips

2 green onions, chopped

2 tbsp. chopped Italian parsley, and extra for garnish

1 tbsp. chopped fresh thyme

Sherry Wine Vinaigrette (p. 183)

Red leaf or Boston lettuce

6 ripe gaeta or ligurian olives, halved and pitted

6 green olives, halved and pitted

Lemon slices for garnish

Drop shrimp into a pot of boiling salted water, cooking 2 to 5 minutes after water returns to boil (timing depends on size of shrimp; test after 2 minutes). Remove with a slotted spoon, shell and devein; set aside. Add lemon juice to boiling water; simmer scallops 2 minutes; drain, quarter and set aside. In a shallow, covered saucepan over high heat, shake-cook mussels until shells open; give clams same treatment. (Discard any unopened shells.) Pry meat from shells, being careful to remove grit, and set aside. Toss prepared shellfish, red pepper, onions and herbs in vinaigrette. Let flavors mingle at room temperature, covered, about 1 hour. (Refrigerate if marinating longer.) Center shellfish on lettuce leaves. Garnish with olives, parsley and lemon slices. Serves 4 to 6.

A Mess of Shellfish

Scrub shells of fresh oysters, clams and/or mussels, allowing 5 or more per serving. Arrange shellfish on the grill over a bed of medium-hot coals. When they begin to open (after about 3 minutes), turn them over and continue cooking until the shells open wide. Provide diners with a small pot of warm melted butter on a plate. Have on hand salt, pepper, lemon wedges, hot crisp bread and piles of napkins.

Sherry Wine Vinaigrette
1 clove garlic, minced
1/4 tsp. salt
2 tbsp. sherry wine vinegar
1 tbsp. lemon juice
1 cup light extra virgin olive oil
Freshly ground pepper

Mash garlic with salt; mix into vinegar and lemon juice. Gradually whisk in oil. Season with pepper to taste.
Makes about 1 cup.

CLAMS

I N THE SEA OF BENTHIC COMPARISONS, A MUSSEL IS ALWAYS a mussel, and preferably eaten cooked; the clam is more varied in size (from thumbnail ones in Japan to the giants of the Indian Ocean, weighing up to 500 lb.), in taste and in treatment (on their own, steamed or otherwise cooked with the sauce of choice, or raw, which many consider the best of all).

To arrive at this variety, not exactly Heinzian, has taken the clam some time. This isn't an organism that likes to be hurried. And why should it be? It's older than we are—about 450 million years older—and look where hurry has got *us*.

It lives a quiet, clean, self-filtering existence, sucking in water and food particles through one valve, expelling them through the other, and left to itself will live perhaps 10 methodical years—unless interrupted by the hurried hungry rest of us (not including Orthodox Jews, whose dietary laws permit only those sea-dwellers bearing scales and fins). Its heartbeat is enviably slow, ranging from two per minute when it's curled up with a good book, to about 20 when it's doing aerobics.

An elemental form of life, then, but one that played a key part, now mostly forgotten, in the opening up of eastern Canada and the northeastern U.S. For years, clams were a specifically North American food—popularized in France, for instance, by Americans as late as World War I—and for centuries, as nature's own mint, they were the basis for wampum: beads made from quahog and cherrystone shells, strung on strands and used for currency by Indians and Europeans alike. (Hence, and also mostly forgotten, the subsequent widespread use of clams as a jocular word for dollars.) This was the wampum so casually traduced in old Hollywood westerns—"Heap big wampum, pale face!"—yet it was used efficiently in trading, without benefit of official sanction, until well into the nineteenth century.

CLAMS CATAPLANA

The name derives from the hinged metal clam-shaped dish in which Portuguese cook and serve them in the Algarve.

36 littleneck clams

2 medium onions, thinly sliced

3 tbsp. olive oil

1 tsp. paprika

1/4 tsp. piri-piri sauce or crushed hot red pepper flakes

Salt and freshly ground pepper

3 medium tomatoes, peeled seeded and chopped
   (or equivalent canned)

8 oz. chorizo sausage, sliced into rounds

2 oz. presunto, prosciutto or smoked ham, chopped

1 bay leaf, crumbled

2 cloves garlic, minced

1/2 cup dry white wine

1/4 cup chopped Italian parsley

Piri-Piri Sauce
Seed and finely chop 1 piri-piri or other small fresh ripe hot red pepper. Place in a small jar and cover with olive oil. Seal tightly and store in a cool place at least a month. Dash into sauces and salad dressing, or brush on fish or meat for the grill.

Scrub clams under cold running water, then soak in lightly salted cold water an hour or so to disgorge any sand; rinse thoroughly. In a large saucepan, cook onions in oil until soft. Stir in paprika, piri-piri and pepper; cook a few minutes, then add remaining ingredients. Simmer 15 minutes. Tuck in clams, hinged side down, and cook, tightly covered, over moderate heat about 10 minutes, shaking pot occasionally across heat; discard clams that don't open. Sprinkle generously with extra parsley and serve with a crusty baguette.
Serves 4.

Desserts

APPLES

"GOD ALMIGHTY FIRST PLANTED A GARDEN," FRANCIS Bacon began one of his famous essays, with the kind of spare, distilled elegance that all writers, no matter how low their station, might well seek to emulate—if in vain, causing them to go back to the source: "God Almighty first planted a garden, and indeed it is the purest of human pleasures." And into the garden he inserted man, woman, serpent and apple, of which two in particular have been causing nothing but grief ever since.

The apple, however, has developed a resoundingly good press over the centuries—doubly surprising in that it was the vehicle for Eden's loss of innocence, but has become the ultimate innocence symbol of the kitchen. Mom's apple pie is still the benchmark of wholesomeness in egregiously unwholesome times; and when was a villain ever described as "apple-cheeked"?

History relates that Ramses III planted apple trees by the thousand in the twelfth century BC along the Nile Valley—perhaps by way of counteracting the exceptional lack of innocence of his wife, Tiy, who sought for years to overthrow him in favor of their son. Only the incurably romantic, though, would ascribe her ultimate failure to the pervasive aura of the apples.

Nearer our time, apples were brought to America by the colonists 400 years ago, and every schoolchild must have heard of Johnny Appleseed (John Chapman), the eccentric missionary who wandered from Pennsylvania to Ohio in the early 1800s, sowing apple seeds along the way as a means of encouraging people to plant orchards.

The legend does not add, alas, that since the best apples come from grafted trees, none of Appleseed's trees—so far as is known—ever bore edible fruit. Less storied but much luckier was Father Pandosy, another missionary, who in 1861 built a church outside Kelowna, B.C., in the Okanagan Valley and surrounded it with apple trees, some of whose offspring are today part of Kelowna's $200-million-a-year crop.

Luckiest of all was John McIntosh, a Scottish American who emigrated to Dundela, Ontario, in 1796, and there found an abandoned apple orchard that had reverted to the wild. Transplanting 20 seedlings, he must have indulged a few mutinous thoughts about Nature when 19 of them keeled over and died. Number 20, however, survived and after eight years began producing spectacular fruit.

They took some time getting to the marketplace. Knowing more about business than horticulture, McIntosh sold seedlings from the parent tree for decades—all of which suffered the same fate as those first 19. Finally, in 1835, a peddler happened by and instructed McIntosh on the grafting arts known to Greeks for some three thousand years, and so enabled the Scot to reap the benefits of his happy accident in the end.

And the original twentieth tree? Badly burned in 1893, it continued bearing fruit until 1906. Today the McIntosh accounts for *half* of all apples sold in North America and a tenth of all sold in the world (from some 7,000 varieties). Not bad for a seedling that made it against all the odds except those of God Almighty, even though a large part of its commercial success must be due less to flavor—other apples have much more—than to its physical beauty, immortalized in North American still lifes for much of the 19th century.

But all the beauty in the world has not enabled any apple—the largest fruit crop in the world—to *transfer* well,

Two items of apple folklore:
(1) To see one's future mate one must stand before a mirror in a darkened room and eat an apple in front of it at midnight. The face of the future mate will appear over the shoulder.
(2) If you can break an apple in half, you can have anyone you choose as your mate for life.
In other words, try (2) before (1).

which is why, more than most fruit, they should be eaten fresh—directly off the tree if you have one handy or have the energy to seek one out; and why, until quite recently, you could never buy apple ice cream.

This last was considered such a profitable untapped market that scientists came up with a synthetic apple taste. And here it is: geranyl valerale, geranyl N-butyrate, geranyl propionate, linalyl formate, isoamyl valerate, vanillin, allyl caprylate, geranyl aldehyde, acetaldehyde, methylcyclopenanalone valerate, alphamethyl furyl acrolein and iso-amyl butyrate.

You will be saying, that's all very well, but in what proportions? Maybe not even God Almighty knows. After all, when He first planted a garden He did not sow the ground with geranyl N-butyrate, perhaps failing to find the butyrates among the purest of human pleasures.

First of all, paint apples and peaches in a fruit bowl.
—Auguste Renoir's counsel on how to capture the particular hues of a woman's breast.

APPLE ALMOND CRUNCH

2 lb. tart apples, peeled and sliced

1/2 cup sugar

1/4 cup Calvados

Pinch salt

Juice of 1/2 lemon

2-inch piece cinnamon stick

2 tbsp. unsalted butter

Almond Crunch (*recipe follows*)

In a large, lidded skillet, combine apples, sugar, Calvados, salt, lemon juice; insert cinnamon stick, and dot with butter. Cook, covered, over medium heat until tender. Remove cinnamon, place apples in a buttered casserole and cover with half the crunch. Bake at 400°F

for 10 minutes. Add remaining crunch, and bake another 10 minutes. Serve warm or at room temperature with whipped cream flavored with a splash of Calvados.
Serves 4 to 6.

Almond Crunch

1/2 cup almonds, blanched and chopped

1/3 cup sugar

1/2 cup all-purpose flour

Pinch salt

4 tbsp. chilled unsalted butter

1/2 tsp. vanilla extract

1 tbsp. Calvados

Combine almonds, sugar, flour, and salt in a large bowl. Cut in butter to form small chunks. (This may be done in a food processor.) Stir in vanilla and Calvados.

Variation: Three Fruit Crunch
Substitute raspberries, pitted black cherries and peeled and sliced peaches for apples, or combine the whole lot, apples and all.

Pears

I T DOESN'T SEEM JUST, BUT THE PEAR IS OUTSOLD BY THE apple in our society, at a ratio of one to ten. The apple, for all its bland apple-pie image, has had dramatic notices since the Garden of Eden: Paris's gift of one to Aphrodite, precipitating the Trojan War; William Tell shooting one off his son's noggin; another falling, knocking the law of gravity into Isaac Newton's; and a few years ago the chemical alar, used in commercial apple orchards, removed from sale by the manufacturer on the advice of Meryl Streep. And the pear? The high point of its 4,000-year career to date is its unflattering inclusion in the epithet *"pear-shaped."*

The modern trouble with the pear lies in the fact that the world is storage and shelf-life crazy and the apple outclasses it on both counts. Pears are easily bruised when ripe: at their very best they can look unappetizingly as if Roseanne Arnold had been using them for worry beads. They also become mealy if allowed to ripen on the tree, which is why commercially they are picked unripe and too often ignored in supermarkets because of it.

Europe, whence our pears came some 300 years ago, has been more hospitable to them than we have ever been. None more so than that high-noon monarch Louis XIV of France, before whom pears were mainly used for cooking.

Because of his encouragement, pears became the supreme fresh fruit of the Age of Reason. Indeed, an excessive attraction to the pear—a pear fetish, perhaps—was key (for males) to getting ahead in the Sun King's entourage. New pear varieties were introduced at court, and Jean de La Quintinie, a lawyer who became head gardener for all Louis's estates, cultivated one strain (La Royale) that produced fruit weighing 2 pounds apiece. One can understand why Louis wrote to La Quintinie's widow after his death: "Madame, you and I have suffered a loss which cannot be recovered."

PEAR CHARLOTTE WITH CARAMEL

Food trends may come and go, but there's always a place for the occasional rich, sweet and boozy dessert flavored, naturally, with the fruits of the season.

1 cup sugar

4 pears, peeled, cored and sliced

2 envelopes (2 tbsp.) unflavored gelatin

1/3 cup Poire William

2 egg whites

1 1/2 cups 35% cream

20 ladyfingers

1/2 cup pieces of praline (*recipe follows*) or toasted
   slivered almonds

Caramel Sauce (*recipe follows*)

In a large saucepan, dissolve 3/4 cup sugar in 1 1/2 cups water; simmer 5 minutes. Add pears; poach until tender. Lift fruit from syrup with a slotted spoon; purée in a food processor or blender, or pass through a sieve. Soften gelatin in 1/4 cup water; stir into purée. Stir in Poire William. Refrigerate until lightly gelled. Whisk egg whites with 1/4 cup sugar until stiff. Beat cream to form soft peaks. Gently but thoroughly fold egg whites and cream into pear gelatin. Line bottom of an 8-cup mold with a circle of waxed paper. Arrange ladyfingers around edge, cementing them together with a dab of pear mixture. Pile pear mixture into mold, cover with a circle of wax paper and refrigerate 6 hours or overnight. To serve, turn out onto a chilled plate, garnish with praline and drizzle with Caramel Sauce.
Serves 8 to 10.

Praline
1/2 cup sugar
2 tbsp. water
1/2 cup chopped almonds, lightly toasted

Boil sugar and water in a small saucepan until sugar turns nutty brown. Stir in almonds. Turn out onto a baking sheet and cool. Break into pieces.
Makes 1/2 cup.

Caramel Sauce
3/4 cup sugar
1/4 cup water
3/4 cup table cream

In a small saucepan, combine sugar and water. Swirl over medium heat until sugar dissolves, then leave to bubble until sugar turns a nutty brown. (Watch that it doesn't burn, or the taste will be bitter.) Carefully add cream (it will steam and bubble furiously) and whisk vigorously until smooth. Serve chilled.
Makes 1 cup.

RASPBERRIES

WHAT CAN ONE SAY ABOUT THE RASPBERRY THAT IS not essentially superfluous, possibly tautologous and almost certainly gratuitous? All we really want to do—should there be naysayers here and there, let them give their share to us—is variously to glory in them, wallow in them, stuff them into ourselves until we can take no more and at the last rub them madly all over our naked bodies.

The Roman emperor Heliogabalus would have understood. That teenaged voluptuary, more fun to read about at a safe distance of 1,770 years than he must have been to live under, once gigglingly suffocated his banquet guests under a few tons of rose petals he had thoughtfully concealed in a trick ceiling. If only he had done the same with raspberries— a member of the rose family, after all—history might have considered him more gently. Surely his guests would have.

But one digresses. It should also be recorded that raspberries come in other colors beside red (white, yellow, black, purple); that commercial red raspberries come from one or another of some 40 forms of the European *Rubus idaeus*, taking its name from the nymph Ida, who pricked her finger while picking white raspberries for the young Jupiter; that fossils near Swiss lakes indicate that raspberries flourished in the cantons several centuries before Christ; that North American Indians have long brewed teas from the raspberry's twigs, leaves and roots to encourage the flow of the kidneys and to stem the flow of dysentery; that respected herbalists still recommend raspberries to pregnant women as the means to avert miscarriage, ease labor pains and increase milk supply; that raspberries have been found superbly efficacious in ridding the body of menstrual cramps, worms and excess fat; that as well as being a source of phosphorus, calcium and vitamins A, B and C, they are also strong in pectin (thus a splendid fruit for jams, jellies, preserves); that they flourish in places with a fine balance of rain and sun; that in late winter, when the northern part of this continent is short of both, New Zealand rasps have been known to fetch $9 a half pint; and that they have not yet been hailed as a cure for cancer.

They will never be cheap to buy. They are too quickly frost-damaged, far too easy prey for such predators as squirrels, raccoons and starlings, too slow and painful (the thorns! the thorns!) to harvest in bulk.

The solution for anyone with a few square feet out back otherwise given over to crabgrass and the excavations of cats: grow one's own. The Heritage strain, developed in the sixties by the New York State Agriculture Experimental Station at Geneva, N.Y., is particularly recommended for home gardeners. A dozen canes planted two feet apart don't need much work to cultivate, cost less than $15, produce a feast of berries the year after planting—and produce them twice, first in mid-July, later from the end of August or until the first frost.

With a little patience, then, the home kitchen would have much to gain. Only things left to worry about would be the squirrels, raccoons and starlings, and what are they beside the end product?

The flavor of the raspberry stamps it Made in Asia. It breathes of the Orient—rich, exotic, spice-laden and with a hint of musk.

RASPBERRY TORTE

This makes a spectacular presentation. The cream cheese and sour cream filling has the lush tartness of crème fraîche.

12 oz. cream cheese, softened

2 tbsp. lemon juice

2 tbsp. sugar

1 cup sour cream

2 9-inch Génoise cakes (*recipe follows*)

4 cups raspberries

Beat cream cheese with lemon juice, sugar and sour cream until smooth. Cut cakes in half horizontally to make four layers. Spread each layer with one-quarter of cream cheese mixture and sprinkle with 1 cup berries. Refrigerate at least 1 hour before serving.

Génoise

A good basic white cake for all manner of fruit toppings or icings.

6 eggs

3/4 cup sugar

1 cup all-purpose flour

1/2 cup unsalted butter, melted and slightly cooled

1 tsp. vanilla extract

1 tsp. grated lemon rind

Combine eggs and sugar in a large bowl, beating lightly with a fork. Place bowl over a pot of simmering water and, stirring gently, heat mixture until it is just warm. Using an electric beater or whisk, beat warmed mixture until it has tripled in volume and resembles whipped cream, 10 to 15 minutes. Sprinkle flour on top and fold in carefully. Gently fold in butter, vanilla and lemon rind. Pour into two greased and floured 9-inch round cake pans. Bake at 350°F until firm, about 30 minutes. Remove cakes from pans and cool on racks.

FRESH FRUIT CRISP

2 cups chopped rhubarb.

1 cup raspberries

1 cup chopped mango or peaches

1/4 cup sugar

1 1/4 tsp. cinnamon

1 tbsp. lemon juice

2 tbsp. dark rum or brandy

1/2 cup all-purpose flour

1/2 cup brown sugar

Pinch salt

1/4 tsp. nutmeg

1/2 cup unsalted butter, cubed

3/4 cup rolled oats

1 cup toasted chopped walnuts, pecans or almonds

Sweetened whipped cream

Toss rhubarb, raspberries and mangoes gently with sugar, 1 tsp. cinnamon, lemon juice and rum. In a separate bowl, combine flour, brown sugar, salt, nutmeg and remaining 1/4 tsp. cinnamon; cut butter into mixture until crumbly; stir in oats and nuts. Spoon fruits into a lightly buttered shallow 8-inch square baking dish. Top with oat mixture. Bake at 350°F for about 40 minutes, until crisp and golden. Garnish with lashings of whipped cream.
Serves 4.

Whipping Cream

To help whip cream to high, stable peaks—no easy feat in these days of homogenization and a witches' brew of additives—add a few drops of lemon juice. The acid slightly modifies the protein but does not alter the taste. Remember: fresh cream will not whip well, warm cream not at all. For best results the whipping cream should be at least one day old and chilled. Also chill the beaters and the bowl. Beat until the cream starts to thicken, then add such sugars and flavoring as will drive sane persons mad.

BLUEBERRIES

ONE OR TWO NOTES ABOUT THE BLUEBERRY, NATURE'S most nearly perfect morning food when plucked ripe from the first country bush, and packed with vitamins and fiber no matter what name it goes by.

Nature's most nearly perfect morning food. A more than usually subjective view, backed only by empirical observation that for some reason as yet unknown to science the blueberry is at its absolute best early in the day. The near-perfection grows unaccountably less near as the day progresses: blueberries at dinner, good as they are, make one wonder if time is out of whack. That's blueberries fresh, but even in blueberry pie, they seem better at noon than after the sun is over the yardarm.

Plucked ripe from the first country bush. Country bush simply refers to lowbush (one to two feet), or wild blueberries; they are notably smaller than the highbush (six to eight feet) cultivated variety; also tarter and more complex in taste. Still, highbush blueberries are not to be sneezed at: these are the ones we buy, frozen, throughout the year, and the ones to be found at pick-your-own farms. Surprisingly, blueberries—which now rank second in North American berry sales to the strawberry—have been cultivated only since the early 1900s.

Packed with vitamins and fiber. A and C, a little B, loaded with calcium.

No matter what name. Close cousins to, and often identified as, bilberries and whortleberries (in Europe), blueberries originated in North America. In the Southern states they are often called huckleberries, which grow only wild and are distinguished from the blues in other parts of the country by larger, hassle-inducing seeds. Mark Twain knew what he was doing: Blueberry Finn just doesn't cut it.

Blueberries as big as the end of your thumb, Real sky-blue, and heavy, and ready to drum In the cavernous pail of the first one to come!
—Robert Frost, on picking your own.

BLUEBERRY CRÈME BRÛLÉE

Annie and David Gringrass serve an exceptional crème brûlée with fruit at Wolfgang Puck's Postrio in San Francisco. This is our adaptation.

6 egg yolks

1/2 cup sugar

3 cups 35% cream

1 vanilla bean, split

3 slices fresh ginger, peeled

2 strips orange rind

7 tbsp. unsalted butter, softened, in pieces

Blueberries in Liqueur (*recipe follows*)

1/2 cup brown sugar

Fluxes are cured now and then by taking a spoonful of Blaeberries.
—From a Scottish medical treatise, 1703.

Whisk yolks and sugar in a bowl set over barely simmering water until thickened enough to form a pale yellow ribbon when poured from a spoon, about 10 minutes. Remove from heat; gradually whisk in cream. Stir in vanilla, ginger and orange peel. Set bowl over barely simmering water, cooking slowly about 45 minutes, stirring frequently until mixture coats back of a wooden spoon. Do not let water boil—on pain of lumps. Remove from heat; whisk in butter, bit by bit; strain. Spoon berries into six 1-cup ramekins, topping with custard; chill 6 hours. Sieve a 1/8-inch layer brown sugar over custard. Place as close as possible to hot broiler 2 minutes to caramelize, watching constantly to avoid burning. Chill again, and concentrate your thoughts on the joy ahead.
Serves 6.

Blueberries in Liqueur

2 cups blueberries

2 tbsp. orange liqueur

2 tbsp. sugar

Toss ingredients together; let stand 20 minutes.

FRESH FRUIT COULIS

Coulis is a straightforward purée of fresh fruit, here spiked with a liqueur, which offers many possibilities for a refreshing dessert sauce: spooned onto ice cream, over cheesecake or into bowls of fruit.

4 cups berries or chopped fresh fruit

2 tbsp. orange liqueur or rum

2 tbsp. lemon or lime juice

Fruit sugar to taste

Purée fruit in food processor with liqueur, lemon juice and sugar. Chill well. If wanting an absolutely clear sauce, press through a sieve; if wanting a thicker one, whisk 2 tsp. cornstarch in 1/4 cup purée, then add to remaining strained purée; cook over medium heat 5 minutes until clear and lightly thickened.
Makes 4 cups.

Give me books, fruit, French wine, fine weather and a little music out of doors, played by some-body I do not know.
—John Keats, 1819.

BLUEBERRY BREAD PUDDING

1 crusty baguette or sweet challah, in 1-inch pieces

3 cups whole milk

1 cup sugar

Pinch each cinnamon and nutmeg

2 cups fresh blueberries

6 eggs

Soak bread in milk at least 30 minutes. Mix in sugar, spices and blueberries. Whisk eggs, stir into mixture, then pour into a buttered 10-inch springform pan. Bake at 350°F about 1 hour until a cake tester inserted near center comes out clean. Cool slightly before unmolding.
Serves 8.

CHOCOLATE

THE GLORIOUS ADDICTIVENESS OF GOOD CHOCOLATE seduces the psyche, wrecks the teeth and lays waste to time. Montezuma, the sixteenth century Aztec emperor, used to sip from 50 golden goblets of the stuff every day, and sip, and sip. He seldom stopped, either from addiction or his belief that chocolate was a potent aphrodisiac. Finally, assassination stopped him, the fatal slip 'twixt cup and lip.

The cocoa tree seems to have developed around the Amazon and Orinoco river systems of South America, and the migrating Aztecs, who learned the chocolate arts from the Maya, brought it north to Mexico about 1,300 years ago. For centuries they used the cocoa bean as currency, the nearest equivalent Central America had to the gold standard (the gold they used for decoration; they found it hard to understand the conquistadors' lust for it).

H.H. Bancroft (1832–1918), American historian and copious writer on Central American matters, reported that while an Aztec pumpkin might cost four cocoa beans and a rabbit could set you back ten, a "tolerably good" slave would cost you as much as 25 pumpkins would. The services of an Aztec lady of pleasure, on the other hand, could be had for the cost of a rabbit.

In the fullness of time the cocoa bean—never the tree itself, which flourishes only in a narrow strip around the Equator—was introduced to Europe by the Spaniards, then by the Dutch. Thence, as with much else, it returned to the New World (northern division) mostly in solid form: the chocolate bar was invented by Britain's Fry and Sons in 1847, milk chocolate in 1875 by Daniel Peter, a Swiss, whose business enterprise was swallowed in a gulp by Nestlé in 1929.

Yes, of course chocolate lies heavy on the calorie scale. But as well as 1,600 calories, a 12-oz. bar will also give us calcium, phosphorus, potassium and bits of vitamins D and E. Most of the beans in it will now have come not from the Americas but from Africa, the new epicenter of the cocoa trade. Spain, which pinched the idea from Montezuma and had a hammerlock on the world's chocolate trade for more than a century, has lost it all.

Montezuma's revenge.

Cooking with it: Be careful how you melt it. Overheating causes pure chocolate to bind and solidify. First, break chocolate into small pieces and set in a bowl over hot—not boiling—water (or use a double boiler). Stir occasionally while it melts; this is about as thrilling as watching paint flake, but your patience will be rewarded.

If impatience sets in and the chocolate starts looking like burned cement, quickly beat in 1 tsp. vegetable oil per ounce of chocolate, and remember we warned you. Also be sure the melting bowl is dry in the first place, and melt away from steam. It takes only a few drops of water to make chocolate grainy.

In 1675 the splendid but mercurial Madame de Sévigné opined in one of her 1,500 letters that chocolate, "like Racine, will go out of fashion very quickly."

In 1900 Milton Snavely Hershey, 43, sold his caramel factory and turned his attention to chocolate. "Caramels are a fad," he announced. "Chocolate is a permanent thing."

Which is why Milton S. is remembered for his Hershey bar and Madame de Sévigné for 1,499 other letters.

CHOCOLATE MARQUISE

Even the strongest will swoon after the first bite, so portion prudently and provide the relief of raspberry coulis.

1/2 lb. bittersweet chocolate

6 egg yolks

1 tsp. instant espresso powder, dissolved in 1/4 cup hot water

2 tbsp. honey

2 tbsp. Apricot Glaze (*see below*)

1/2 cup unsalted butter

1/2 cup sugar

1/2 cup cocoa powder

1 cup 35% cream, whipped to soft peaks

Melt chocolate in a bowl set over simmering water. Whisk in yolks, espresso, honey and apricot glaze. Cream butter with sugar and cocoa until smooth; fold into chocolate. Fold in whipped cream. Pour into a 9- x 5-inch loaf pan lined with plastic wrap and let set in refrigerator 24 hours. To serve; unmold, remove plastic wrap and slice.
Serves 15.

Tip: This freezes well.

Apricot Glaze
Combine 1 cup apricot jam with 2 tbsp. lemon juice in a small saucepan. Simmer and stir for a couple of minutes until smooth. Press through a sieve. Store in refrigerator until needed.

Tiramisù

There are as many versions of Italy's pick-me-up as there used to be stars at MGM.

1/4 cup strong coffee

1/2 cup coffee liqueur

20 ladyfingers

4 eggs, separated

1 lb. mascarpone (*see sidebar*)

1/2 cup sugar

4 1-oz. squares semisweet chocolate, grated

2 cups Fresh Fruit Coulis, using raspberries (*see p. 200*)

1 cup fresh berries (raspberries, strawberries, blueberries)

Blend coffee with 1/4 cup liqueur; brush ladyfingers on both sides. Neatly line the bottom and sides of a shallow dish (2 1/2 inches deep); reserve 8 ladyfingers. Beat egg yolks until smooth and slightly thickened. Blend in mascarpone and remaining 1/4 cup liqueur. Whisk whites until stiff, gradually adding sugar. Fold gently but firmly into cheese mixture. Spoon half of this luscious mixture onto ladyfingers. Top with half the grated chocolate, then remaining cheese mixture, then remaining chocolate. Cover and chill overnight. Spoon into serving dishes. Surround with coulis and scatter berries over all. For absolute overkill, whipped cream may be piped on top.
Serves 6.

Mascarpone
A decadent cheese with a rich creamy texture and sweet delicate taste. Used in much the same way as you would use heavy cream, with fruits and in desserts.

TULIPES

A tulip of crisp cookie makes a delightful container for serving an ice. The batter is similar to the one used for langues de chats. (Pictured opposite page 152.)

1/4 cup unsalted butter, softened

1/2 cup sugar

2 egg whites

Dash vanilla extract

1/2 cup all-purpose flour

Melted chocolate (optional)

Cream butter and sugar until light. Mix in egg whites and vanilla. Fold in flour. Line baking sheets with parchment paper, and draw circles 5 to 6 inches in diameter (two to four will fit on a standard tray). Spread a very thin layer of batter to fill each circle. Bake at 350°F for 6 to 8 minutes. Keep cookies waiting in oven with door ajar. To form tulipe, turn jar upside down and lightly oil bottom and sides. Quickly lift a just-baked cookie from sheet, place over jar, and let fall down sides to shape. Remove and let it sit in a cup or muffin tin to cool. All this is a hideous task and will leave you with many broken cookies plus a good dose of frustration; but bear in mind the results are well worth it. Inside of cooled tulipes may be brushed or drizzled with melted chocolate.
Makes 12.

Glazed Tangerines

8 tangerines

1 cup water

1 cup white wine

1 cup sugar

1 sprig rosemary

2 tbsp. lemon juice

Squeeze juice from 2 tangerines. Peel remaining tangerines, removing pith from peel and cutting them into fine strips; carefully remove pith from sections. Combine tangerine juice, water, wine, sugar and rosemary in a pot; bring to a boil, and simmer until clear and lightly thickened (about 10 minutes). Add tangerines, lemon juice, poaching gently 10 to 15 minutes over medium heat; lift out with a slotted spoon, placing in a shallow dish with 1 cup poaching liquid; chill well. Stir peel into pot, and simmer briskly until transparent (about 10 minutes); cool peel on a rack. Place tangerines in individual dishes or chocolate-brushed tulipe cups, garnishing with peel.
Serves 6.

BLACK GRAPE GRANITA

A superbly refreshing restorative. (Pictured opposite page 153.)

1 1/2 lb. black grapes

1/2 cup sugar

1/2 cup water

Juice of 1 orange

1/4 cup port or sweet white wine

Fresh mint for garnish

Halve grapes and purée, skins and all. In a small saucepan, combine sugar and water; boil 5 minutes to make a syrup. After cooling, stir into grape purée. Strain mixture. Flavor with orange juice. Pour into a metal freezer tray or bowl. Freeze 2 to 3 hours, stirring occasionally and scraping frozen edges to center. When quite firm, break up and beat in port with a hand mixer. Freeze again 1 hour, until mixture forms a nice slush. Spoon into glasses or tulipes. Garnish with fresh mint.
Serves 6.

CITRUS MANGOES WITH GINGER ICE CREAM

Mangoes should be firm but not hard and the aroma should be strong. This dessert is tartly refreshing.

4 mangoes

2 tbsp. grated fresh ginger

Juice of 2 limes (4 tbsp.)

Finely grated rind of 2 limes

1 tbsp. finely minced candied ginger

1 tbsp. finely chopped mint

Ginger Ice Cream (*recipe follows*)

Peel mangoes. Carefully slice fruit into strips. Squeeze juice from grated ginger. Combine ginger juice, lime juice and grated lime rind with mangoes. Toss well and chill. Arrange slices of mango on plates. Sprinkle with candied ginger and a little chopped mint. Serve with Ginger Ice Cream and a chocolate-dipped biscuit. For a spectacular presentation, serve ice cream in chocolate-glazed tulipes.
Serves 4.

Ginger Ice Cream

1 cup 18% cream

1/2 vanilla bean, cut in half lengthwise

5 egg yolks

1/2 cup sugar

2 slices fresh ginger, peeled

1 strip orange rind

2 tbsp. ginger syrup

1/2 cup 18% cream

1/2 cup 35% cream

2 tbsp. finely chopped candied ginger

Heat 1 cup 18% cream and vanilla bean until cream is hot; do not let it boil. Beat egg yolks and sugar until smooth, thick and a creamy yellow. Discard vanilla bean; gradually add hot cream to egg mixture. Return to the heat, add fresh ginger and orange rind; cook over low heat, stirring constantly, until the mixture, which will resemble a custard, thickens enough to coat a spoon, about 10 minutes. Remove from the heat, strain and let cool. Stir in the remaining cream and ginger syrup. Pour into an ice-cream maker and freeze according to manufacturer's instructions. Fold in candied ginger partway through freezing.
Makes 1 pint.

Tip: Candied ginger with syrup is available in jars.

Serenely full, the Epicure would say,
Fate cannot harm me, I have dined today.
—Rev. Sydney Smith (1771-1845)

Glossary

ASIAN INGREDIENTS

Fish Sauce
A salty clear brown sauce with a terrible aroma that imparts a wonderful distinctive taste to prepared dishes. Made from small fish, salted and packaged in wooden barrels.

Five-Spice Powder
A blend usually containing ground star anise, fennel, cinnamon, cloves and ginger. Better prepared yourself, but available packaged, usually found with dried peppers.

Fresh Ginger
Fresh ginger, a rough brown rhizome that often looks like a hand, is readily available these days. To use, peel, grate and squeeze, reserving juice. Add juice to sauces, salad dressings or steamed vegetables. Fresh, peeled and sliced ginger is excellent added to oil for a stir fry or to a soup. Slice and smash for stocks (chicken or fish) or marinade.

Garam Masala
A blend of ground spices—cardamom, cinnamon, cloves, peppercorns, cumin and coriander. Used to add flavoring to dishes at the end of cooking.

Hoisin Sauce
A sweet thick mahogany-colored sauce. Made from soy beans, garlic and chilis. Sold in jars. Excellent in marinades.

Hot Chili Paste
A fresh red chili paste purchased as sambal oelek (Go Tan from Holland) or the Vietnamese Tuong Ot Toi from Huy Fong. Substitute 1 tsp. to 1 tbsp very finely minced red or green fresh chilies.

Krupuck/Shrimp Chips
These shrimp chips are flat, small and translucent. They puff up to 4 times their size when deep-fried. Fry in 1-inch peanut or corn oil in bottom of large skillet: they cook instantly (don't let them brown). Serve with any curry dish or as a snack. Our preference: Shanghai Prawn Crackers Factory, People's Republic of China (in a blue box with a large prawn on it).

Lemongrass
Looks like a dried green onion. The coarse bulb is sliced and added to soups, stews and marinades. It has a sharp lemon taste, wonderfully fragrant.

Lime Leaves or Kaffir
Oval olive green leaves. Available dried, though fresh are now more readily available. Used much like bay leaves. Lend a fragrant, pungent lime/lemon flavor to soups and stews.

Oyster Sauce
Like a thickened soy sauce, flavored with oysters, more delicate. A tablespoon in stir-fries adds excellent flavor.

Pappadums
Flat, dried golden rounds of udad dal flour. Sold in packages of 12, they puff up and double in size when deep-fried. Serve with curries.

Rice Vinegar
A very light, slightly sweet vinegar. Makes wonderful dressings for salad, especially without oil. Marukan brand is the best available.

Saffron
The dried stamens of the crocus. Do not buy ground, as it may not be the real thing. Soak for 5 minutes in cooking broth. To intensify flavor, dry briefly in a warm pan before soaking. The best saffron comes from Spain.

Sesame Oil
Oil extracted from toasted sesame seeds. Buy pure sesame seed oil in glass bottles, such as Kadoya and Y&Y brands. Use sparingly at end of cooking to add flavor as it burns easily. May be mixed with other oil for cooking. Excellent in salads, again, diluted with a milder oil.

Shrimp Paste or Bagoong
Pinkish brown paste made from fermented shrimp, usually sold in jars.

Soy Sauce
Made from fermented salted soy beans. Use Pearl River Superior Soy Sauce (red label) for general use. Try the mushroom soy sauce (gold label) for a heartier version. Japanese soy sauce is lighter and sweeter in taste, best for dressings and fish. Kikkoman is fine to use.

Szechuan Peppercorns
A dark reddish brown seed, delicate and fragrant, not spicy. Toss peppercorns in a heavy skillet over medium heat just to heat through. Cool and grind or crush.

Thai Curry Paste
Red, yellow and green curry pastes, available canned. Namprik Maesri is a good brand. You can make your own but these impart good flavor.

VINEGARS AND OILS

VINEGAR:

Vinegar has been around for thousands of years, most likely originating by accident, the result of wine being left around to oxidize and ferment. Romans and Greeks appreciated sour tastes to enhance appetite, to mask the flavor of foods less than fresh and to add interest to a plain diet.

In Cooking:

Good vinegar has pleasing flavor and acidity (usually between 4 percent and 7 percent). It is carefully made from wine and vinegar and allowed to age in wooden vats where the alcohol changes to acetic acid. To speed up the process in modern times wine is oxidized, diluted, filtered and pasteurized to produce vinegar of eternal shelf life with maximum efficiency—resulting in little flavor and unpleasant harshness.

BALSAMIC VINEGAR:

The aristocrat among vinegars, made for centuries in the region around Modena in Italy. Mellow and rich in flavor, with almost syrupy consistency, much prized even to be a valuable asset in a bride's dowry. Sipped and appreciated much like a fine wine as a restorative! Aged as long as fifty years in wooden barrels. Genuine balsamic is expensive and mostly secreted away by the folks in Modena. Commercial varieties (the process is speeded up; caramelized grape juice is added to wine vinegar with a dash of oak flavoring) range in quality

OILS

Our cupboards usually include a variety: Light vegetable oils (sunflower or canola) for some cooking or dressings; peanut oil, which can be used at higher temperatures without burning, which makes it good for deep-frying or stir-frying; mild fruity extra virgin olive oil from Nyon and a more gutsy extra virgin olive oil from Tuscany or Portugal; walnut and hazelnut oil and sesame oil for dressings and flavoring; a good-quality blended extra virgin olive oil for general cooking. Make your own flavored oils using fresh herbs, garlic or hot peppers.

Index

List of Photographs